MISTER JACK — FOR BETTER OR FOR WORSE

MISTER JACK — FOR BETTER OR FOR WORSE

MARVIN KAYE

WORLD LIBRARY CLASSICS

Published by Wildside Press, LLC.
www.wildsidebooks.com

CONTENTS

INTRODUCTION

MY TWO AFFAIRS WITH DON JUAN

One of our culture's greatest cautionary legends is that of Don Juan, whose unrepentant womanizing was punished when the statue of a vengeful father he killed in a duel came to life and bore the sinner to Hell.

The lascivious hero first appeared on stage in 1630 in the Spanish play *El Burlador de Sevilla*, by Tirso de Molina, and in many guises since then, including a long satiric poem by Lord Byron (in which the English perversely pronounce his name Don Joo-an), a drama by Molière, the Lorenzo Da Ponte libretto for Mozart's opera, *Don Giovanni*, an Ingmar Bergman film, *The Devil's Eye*, as well as the witty "Don Juan in Hell" sequence of Bernard Shaw's theatrical polemic, *Man and Superman*.

It is unfortunate that one of the most imaginative of all Don Juan plays, *La Dernière Nuit de Don Juan,* is virtually unknown, even though it was written by Edmond Rostand (1868—1918), creator of the magnificent French heroic comedy-drama *Cyrano de Bergerac,* as well as *Les Romanesques* (*The Romantics*), on which was based America's longest-running musical, *The Fantasticks.* Understandably patterned on Molière's *Don Juan* (even quoting its final speech), Rostand takes the legend in a direction unusual for a dramatist whose work is considered the last great flowering of French romanticism. In addition to equating the Don Juan myth with that of Punchinello, the playwright undertakes a foray into character dissection that suggests he may have been conversant with Freud . . . they were, after all, contemporaries, and *La Dernière Nuit de Don Juan* was Rostand's final play.

I had heard it was posthumously incomplete, but when I read it both in French and English translation, I thought it finished, so far as its basic plotline is concerned, though perhaps he might have undertaken revisions had he survived.

In the process of adapting the play for The Open Book, New York's oldest (and only) nonprofit readers theatre company, I followed Rostand's own dictum, "All great art must be updated," which he puts into Don Juan's mouth for abridging the Punch-and-Judy show. The cosmetic alterations I made to render the play more accessible to American audiences and readers are as follows:

• I condensed the action from a somewhat verbose two acts with intermission to a brief prologue and three scenes meant to be performed without interruption. I tried not to cut dialogue, preferring instead to tighten it by opting for a fairly simple poetic prose instead of the original's heightened, rhymed verse.

• There are several places in the script that do not flow as congenially as is usual in Rostand; in these spots I have transposed speeches when I thought the progress of idea would therefore run more smoothly and logically.

• Rostand's list of characters calls for 1,003 distaff spectres. In the theatre collection at Lincoln Center, an earlier English translation suggests that fifteen women would be more than sufficient to give the illusion of this vast company of seduced ghosts, but in today's impoverished theatre even that many actresses would be more than most producers' budgets could afford (not to mention the scheduling problems!). Since the puppet theatre is already an integral part of the action, I decided that I could also stylize the spectres by using three and assigning them a variety of multi-colored masks. Thus each of these ghosts represent 334.3 of their sisters-in-damnation.

• The major excision I made was to cut a scene involving a beggar whom Don Juan invokes to prove to the Devil that his imperiled spirit has worth, if not as a lover, than as a blasphemer. This episode refers to a moment in Moliere's *Don Juan* in which a supplicant begs for alms in the name of God only to be given money by Don Juan on the understanding that it is for the love of man and not the deity that he bestows it. Rostand's beggar curses both Don Juan and his money as false coin. I eliminated this sequence because, firstly, the Moliere reference is now obscure, and secondly, it seemed to me an intrusion into a drama whose purpose is to pick apart the Don's sexual pretensions.

Don Juan and The Mid-Day Demon

Though for many years I planned to write a play about the downside of romantic love, I had not perceived that it would be a twist on the Don Juan myth.

Shortly after graduating from Penn State as a graduate student in theatre and English literature, I read an essay, "Accidie," by Aldous Huxley, which dealt with an ancient fiend known as *daemon meridianus*, the only evil spirit unafraid of doing his nefarious work in broad daylight.

In Huxley's words, Accidie, or Acedia, as he was known in English, "would lie in wait for monks grown weary with working in the oppressive heat, seizing a moment of weakness to force an entrance into their hearts . . ." To the hapless victim, his poor life suddenly seemed "desolatingly empty." He would wonder if there was any point to existence. Slowly his spirit would sink "through disgust and lassitude into the black depths of despair and hopeless unbelief." That constituted a good day's work for Accidie.

The concept resonated in me and I wanted to write about it. I planned a trilogy of plays to be collectively called *The Mid-Day Demon*. Each would focus on some social institution and explore the hollowness therein. The first, to be called *We About to Die,* was concerned with temporal power, and the final installment, *The Golden Tears of Zeus,* was intended as a study of the dysfunctional family. I completed a rough draft of the first script; it lays in a drawer unread since the 1970s, when it put its author to sleep.

The middle installment, for which I had no title, would examine romantic and sexual love. After reading and enjoying Bernard Shaw's *Man Into* Superman with its long interlude, "Don Juan in Hell," I began to think about the possibility of making my play a Don Juan comedy.

In 1988, Susan Shwartz asked me to contribute a short story to her "Arabian Nights" anthology, *Arabesques 2* (Avon Books, 1989). I returned to my old theme and complied with "The Tale of Sindbad and the Mid-Day Demon."

Fast-forward now to the 1990's; The Open Book, the theatre company I cofounded in 1975 with Bill Bonham and Saralee Kaye moved into the Amsterdam Room on West 85th Street near Amsterdam Avenue in Manhattan. One of the shows we did in 1994 or '95 was *This Evening Rated 'R.'* It featured a one-act play by Mario Fratti and my own adaptation of the Plautus farce, *Asinaria.*

I looked through my library to find a curtain raiser for the program, and came upon an old British comedy in one act, Alfred Sutro's "The Man in the Stalls."

Though I thought it dated, I liked its story well enough to try my hand at my long-overdue Don Juan play. Using Sutro's plot structure, I wrote "Mister Jack's Off Day."

It played fairly well. I thought, and thought about it . . . and thought about it . . . and many years later, I rewrote it and made it the opening scene of *Mister Jack.*

The Open Book planned to produce my new script a few years ago but when my dear friend and colleague Carole Buggé showed me her superb script, *Strings,* I set my own play aside and produced/directed hers, and am very glad I did; it was one of the best shows The Open Book did in our thirty-five year history.

At length we began working on producing *Mister Jack* in May, 2010, at the 78th Street Theatre Lab, Manhattan, with the following cast:

Leo — H. CLARK KEE
Mister Jack — ERIC ROLLAND
Dana — GIOIA deCARI
Kathleen/Violetta — STACEY JENSON

Don Juan's Final Night was scheduled as an after-piece, with the following cast:

Narrator/The Statue/The Devil — MARVIN KAYE
Sganarelle/Punchinello — H. CLARK KEE
Don Juan — ERIC ROLLAND
A Ghost — GIOIA deCARI
2nd Ghost — JOANNE DORIAN
3rd Ghost — MICHELE PAYNE
The Silver Spirit — STACEY JENSON

— Marvin Kaye
New York, 2010

DON JUAN'S FINAL NIGHT

BY EDMOND ROSTAND

Freely revised and adapted by
MARVIN KAYE

PROLOGUE

DON JUAN *is being led to Hell by* THE STATUE *of the Commander. A sulphurous glow from below lights up the narrow circular staircase that they are descending.*

DON JUAN *(calmly)*

Each step I go down reminds me of a woman I mounted. Jeanette . . . Nanette . . . Laurette . . . Release my arm, old man. I'll enter Hell unassisted.

(Far away, a dog howls.)

Listen! At least my faithful spaniel misses me. But what about my faithful manservant, Sganarelle? Lord Commander, grant me a moment's rest that I may hear him mourn me.

(They pause. The distant sound of SGANARELLE *grumbling.)*

SGANARELLE'S VOICE

His death pleases everyone else: the God he spurned, the laws he flouted, the women he ravished, the families he disgraced, the husbands and lovers he drove to frenzy. But what about me? The only satisfaction I get is to see my master's dreadful punishment. My wages, my wages—ah, my wages![1]

DON JUAN

Will you let me go back to earth long enough to pay him back?

THE STATUE

Yes.

DON JUAN

I'll be eternally grateful. *(He ascends.)*

---

1   Here Rostand quotes the final speech of Moliere's *Don Juan or the Feast of Stone*, in which the great French dramatist employs his perennial comic foil, Sganarelle, instead of Mozart's Italian lackey, Leporello, But in the original Spanish Don Juan play, Tirso de Molina's *The Blasphemer of Seville*, the servant's name is Catalinon. —MK

THE STATUE *(muses)*

I wonder if he'll return.

DON JUAN *(coming back down)*

There! I gave him what he deserves.

THE STATUE

His wages?

DON JUAN

A kick in the ass. He earned it. *(Laughs)* It'll comfort me while I'm roasting.

THE STATUE *(admiringly)*

Nothing frightens you, Don Juan. That stirs pleasant memories in this old warrior's breast. Your courage shall be rewarded. I'm going to let you go. Hurry and climb.

> *(A monstrous claw suddenly clutches* DON JUAN *by the cloak.)*

DON JUAN

You should have thought of that before. It's too late, the Devil's got me.

> *(Cockcrow.)*

THE STATUE

It's almost dawn. I must become mute stone once more. Farewell, Don Juan, I hope you somehow escape the Devil's clutch. *(He ascends.)*

DON JUAN

Well, I'll try. Don't close the tomb yet, maybe I'll get out. *(Tugs his cloak)* Come, Lucifer, let go. Do you really think I've performed all the evil I can do on earth? Let's make a deal. Give me another ten years and I'll surpass your wildest expectations. You'll find me better mettle than that dullard Faust. Imagine being content with one mumpish German fraulein! See my arm where your emissary grasped it? The burning cold of his stone fingers made these scars. Ladies will dote on them. Haven't I always been your vicar of vice? I promise you, in ten more years I shall debauch a thousand virtuous women.

(The great claw disappears.)

Bravo, Don Juan! You've won yourself another decade. *(He starts to mount the steps.)* Annette . . . Minette . . . Lisette . . . Ho, Sganarelle! There's work to do!

(The lights fade out.)

SCENE ONE

Ten years later. A large banquet hall in a Venetian palace. Great marble stairs lead to the Grand Canal and the Adriatic Sea. DON JUAN *descends the steps and enters as* SGANARELLE *sets a candelabra on a table laden for a feast.*

DON JUAN

Arlette . . . Paulette . . . Lynette . . . A grand night on the Grand Canal. The lagoon sleeps beneath skies of purple and sulphur. Tiny craft, like nipples on the bosom of the ocean, streak the sea with trails of milk and silver. *(To* SGANARELLE*)* It's done. Add her name to my list.

SGANARELLE

Whose name? You pursue so many ladies, master, how am I supposed to know which one you mean?

DON JUAN *(holds up a ring)*

Hers. *(He tosses the ring over the balcony into the canal.)*

SGANARELLE *(horrified)*

No! Not the ruby! You promised me that one!

DON JUAN

Of course not, fool. The glass ring. *(He chuckles cynically.)* She was naive.

SGANARELLE *(shocked)*

That lady? I should have thought that she, at least—

DON JUAN *(interrupts)*

Come now, Sganarelle . . . what hope for virtue in a city whose very streets are mirrors? Frailty, thy name is Venice. I adore it here. The gondoliers croon "Santa Lucia" and half my work's accomplished. I won't return to the grey skies of native Spain. Write upon my tombstone that Don Juan was born in Seville but fulfilled his destiny in Venice.

SGANARELLE

Well, since you broach the subject, master . . . your ten years are up this evening. How do you plan to spend your final night?

DON JUAN

How else, but at my favorite pastime?

SGANARELLE

You don't mean to go out again?

DON JUAN

There's a fancy ball. I'll go there and better Hannibal. He merely crossed the Alps, but I will conquer loftier peaks.

SGANARELLE

But afterward you'll come back home?

DON JUAN

Afterward, who knows? Once before, I escaped Lucifer's claw. Perhaps by now he's forgotten us.

SGANARELLE *(alarmed)*

Us? What do you mean, "us"?

DON JUAN

A figure of speech, dolt, don't be nervous; the Devil won't snatch you away for many years. You'll have ample time to enjoy your inheritance.

SGANARELLE *(eagerly)*

My inheritance? Best of masters, what have you left me?

DON JUAN

My reputation. Tell them you worked for the infamous Don Juan and you'll have job offers and mistresses galore.

SGANARELLE *(dubiously)*

How do you figure that?

DON JUAN

Your masters will want you to teach them my methods.

SGANARELLE

What about the mistresses?

DON JUAN

Ladies disappointed that they could not sleep with Don Juan will gladly settle for his servant

SGANARELLE

Master, this braggadocio is all well and good, but it won't help you any when the clock strikes and the Devil hauls you down to Hell

(The hour tolls ominously.)

DON JUAN

Speak of the Devil and hear his voice. Did I keep my bargain? What's the final tally?

SGANARELLE

In the past ten years? One thousand and three. That's certainly enough.

DON JUAN

I'm sorry to stop at an odd number. If I could only add one more name to the roster . . .

(The chiming ceases. A long silence.)

Perhaps Lucifer changed his mind. No, that's not it; the priest Tertullian must be right . . . the Devil is dead. *(With a laugh, he goes briskly to the table.)* Don Juan endures! First I'll sup—then to the ball and other sweetmeats. Sganarelle, fetch my masque and rapier. I'm still master of my destiny.

A DISTANT VOICE

Commedia!

DON JUAN

Hark. The cry of the showman hawking his talents. Life goes on . . . bravo!

THE VOICE *(closer)*

Commedia!

SGANARELLE *(looking over the balcony)*

It's the old puppeteer from the Schiavoni wharf.

DON JUAN

Punch and Judy? Splendid! Tell him to come up here.

SGANARELLE

And do what?

DON JUAN

And put on his play while I dine.

SGANARELLE *(shouting)*

Hey! Old man . . . come along. Here you have a willing audience.

> *(The* MARIONETTE MAS-
> TER *enters, bowing. He wears
> a large hat.)*

MARIONETTE MASTER

A command performance? I'm flattered. Shall I build my little theatre for you?

DON JUAN

Yes, and while you do, tell me where you come from.

MARIONETTE MASTER *(putting up his stage)*

I come from wandering to and fro in the earth and walking up and
down in it. Writers, painters and composers all know me well.

DON JUAN

Then we're kindred spirits, I've traveled far, too. Yet my own legend
outpaces me.

MARIONETTE MASTER

Indeed? Well, in my theatre, you'll see that myth is reduced to miniature.

> *(With a flourish, the* MARI-
> ONETTE MASTER *indicates
> that his stage is ready. He ducks*

*beneath the curtain and is hid-
den.)*

DON JUAN
Behold the Attic temple that first tutored me in the cruelties of existence.

SGANARELLE
Why do you call it a temple, master? It's only a puppet stage. And
we're not in the attic.

DON JUAN
Be off with you, rascal! If I must endure a blockhead, I far prefer it
to be Punch,

> *(SGANARELLE exits. DON
> JUAN begins eating. PUNCH
> pops his head above the stage.
> DON JUAN claps his hands
> like a happy child, but PUNCH
> screams in pretended fright and
> disappears. DON JUAN laughs.
> PUNCH tentatively reappears.)*[2]

PUNCH *(calls)*
Toinette . . . ? Margrette . . . ? Judette . . . ? Oh, Ju-u-dette . . . *(He
sees DON JUAN.)* What? Is it really you, at long last? Hurrah! Hurrah!

DON JUAN
What are you cheering about?

PUNCH
Because I've finally found you, Don Juan, Hurrah!

DON JUAN
Ah, so you know who I am?

PUNCH
Now wouldn't I be the ass if I didn't know my own brother?

---

2   The marionettes should be portrayed by actors. —MK

DON JUAN *(not sure he is amused)*

Your brother? How?

PUNCH

Brothers in degeneracy.

DON JUAN

Don Punch, you always had a wicked tongue.

PUNCH

Don Juan, you always had a profligate spirit. On the Day of Judgment, they'll put us both in the balances and we'll come out even, you'll see.

DON JUAN *(angrily)*

Is that so, you woman beater?

PUNCH

It certainly is, you womanizer.

DON JUAN

Don Punch . . . you are a blockhead!

PUNCH

Don Juan . . . you are my brother!

DON JUAN *(laughs)*

So you claim we're siblings. Am I, then, another marionette?

PUNCH

Nay, no one ever links those syllables, "marry," with the name of Don Juan.

DON JUAN *(smiles)*

Now you're quibbling. I've had a thousand brides, no matter whose. *(Resumes eating)* But take me back to my childhood and the Punch-and-Judy plays I loved to see.

PUNCH

Well, what did you like best about those shows?

DON JUAN

Truthfully? Admiring the ladies in the audience.

PUNCH

And looking up their skirts?

DON JUAN

Never mind that Come, begin. Sing your song.

PUNCH *(warms up vocally)*

La-la-la-la la-la-la-la-a-a-a-a-a-a-a-h-h-h-h-h-h'h-h-h-h!

(Sings)   I'm the famous puppet, Punch.
I love ladies by the bunch.
But I always beat their heads.

> *(DON JUAN raises his wine-glass to PUNCH.)*

DON JUAN *(singing the same tune)*

I'm the blasphemer, Don Juan.
I love ladies with élan.
And I always heat their beds.

> *(They sing together, each repeating his own verse, but just before the final syllable, a puppet of THE COMMANDER appears and interrupts them with his own musical outburst)*

THE COMMANDER[3]

Punchinello, you've ruined my daughter. Now die!

> *(PUNCH fetches his stick and beats the other puppet over the head. THE COMMANDER sings to the Commendatore's*

---

3   Matching the first phrase the Commendatore sings ("*Lasciala, indegno! Battiii meco!*") in Mozart's *Don Giovanni*—MK

Mozartian death phrase. "Ah, soccorso! son tradito , , ,")

THE COMMANDER

Ah, support me! I am dying.

(He disappears under the stage.)

DON JUAN

I've seen this part of the play before. Go on to something else. Call Judy.

PUNCH *(calls)*

Oh-h-h, Ju-u-u-dette . . .

(She promptly appears. PUNCH woos her.)

O, Judette, Judette, Judette . . . I love you!

(She spurns him.)

DON JUAN

Your technique, brother Punch, leaves something to be desired.

PUNCH

What did I do wrong?

DON JUAN

Never start off by telling them you love them. That comes later.

PUNCH

Then what am I supposed to say to her?

DON JUAN

Say nothing. Look remote. Your indifference will cause her pain.

PUNCH

Pain? I already know how to manage that!

(He whacks JUDY with his stick.)

DON JUAN

No, no, no, that's not what I meant. You mustn't strike women. You must make them suffer. There's a difference.

> (PUNCH *picks up the* JUDY PUPPET.)

PUNCH *(indifferently)*

Too late.She's dead.*(He tosses her offstage.)* What do you want to see next? The scene where they sentence me to death?

DON JUAN

No, cut that one.

PUNCH

What about where they hang me?

DON JUAN

No, omit that, too.

PUNCH

Do you realize you're abridging a time-tested plot?

DON JUAN

Time itself must change with the times and all great art must be updated.

PUNCH

But you've skipped over practically my whole story! What's left?

DON JUAN

The part where the Devil carries you off. That's a spectacle I certainly don't want to miss.

PUNCH

Very well.

> *(He strikes a small bell.)*

DON JUAN

What did you ring that for?

PUNCH

Sound effects. It's supposed to be midnight. *(He shakes with fear)* Satan's on his way . . . I'm scared!

> *(*THE DEVIL PUPPET *enters, growling.* PUNCH *swats him.* THE DEVIL PUPPET *snatches away the stick and batters* PUNCH, *then slings* PUNCH *over his left shoulder.* PUNCH *howls piteously as* THE DEVIL PUPPET *disappears offstage with him.)*

DON JUAN

Poor brother Punch . . . you shouldn't have struck the Devil.

THE DEVIL PUPPET *(popping up)*

Perhaps, instead, he should have made me suffer?

DON JUAN

Of course. That's what I'd do.

THE DEVIL PUPPET *(in a different tone)*

Indeed? May one inquire how?

DON JUAN

What happened to your voice?

THE DEVIL PUPPET

It's not important. Come, take me into your confidence. I'm eager to know how you would make me suffer.

DON JUAN

You notice how Punch squealed like a stuck pig? The howl of sinners tossed into the fiery Pit is a sound that pleases you. You'll never hear it from me.

THE DEVIL PUPPET *(sneers)*

It's easy to brag before I have you in my clutches.

DON JUAN

But that's the point. You'll never have me. Not the way you want. The only thing that makes me tremble is lust. I'm called the Blasphemer of Seville. I mock God and Lucifer alike.

THE DEVIL PUPPET

Don Juan, this I promise you . . . you won't go to Hell until I've thoroughly broken your spirit.

DON JUAN

Now that's good news.

THE DEVIL PUPPET *(holding out his claw)*

Here's my hand on it.

> *(*DON JUAN *reaches for the puppet's hand.* THE DEVIL PUPPET *disappears and the* MARIONETTE MASTER *appears in its place and shakes* DON JUAN*'s hand instead.)*

DON JUAN

Your claw is colder than the Commander's stone fist

> *(As* DON JUAN *pulls away his hand, the* MARIONETTE MASTER *throws off his disguise and reveals himself to be* THE DEVIL.*)*

So it's you, Lucifer. I took you for a master of marionettes.

THE DEVIL

Why, so I am, and always have been. This very night I've yanked the strings of senators and kings, beggars and justices, and now it's your turn. Shall I toss you over my shoulder like your brother Punch?

DON JUAN

No, I'll walk on my own two feet. Let's go, I'm ready for Hell. *(He sports himself proudly.)* Caparisoned in tastefully decadent apparel, I'll grace your graceless company. I presume old Charon's still your gondolier?

THE DEVIL

Ever the posturer. I suppose your mistresses expected it. Shall we dine?

(He sits down at the table.)

DON JUAN

If my roast pleases you better than roasting me, so be it.

THE DEVIL

We shook hands, remember?

DON JUAN

You mean unless you daunt my proud spirit, I shall not go to Hell? Then I'm saved.

THE DEVIL

We'll see.

(With DON JUAN *acting as host,* THE DEVIL *helps himself to food and wine and begins to eat and drink.)*

(Appreciatively) You're quite a cook, Don Juan.

DON JUAN

I have to be. It's all part of the art of seduction: sensual cuisine, opulent decor, wine as carefully chosen as every voluptuous word I speak. All must be resplendent. You, however, are decidedly drab. Why do you wear so much black?

THE DEVIL

To match the inkstand Martin Luther hurled at me.

DON JUAN

You look a lot better in green.

THE DEVIL

How do you know that? I haven't worn green—

DON JUAN *(interrupting)*

Since the Garden of Eden. I was there, don't you remember? In those days, I called myself Adam, You got me to eat the apple of knowledge.

THE DEVIL

Admittedly an acquired taste. How did you like it?

DON JUAN

I didn't, there was a worm inside. I threw that apple away and tried another. It also contained a worm. So did the next one and the next. *(Pause)* So does all Creation.

THE DEVIL

Yes, that's the knowledge God tried to hide from you. I spoiled his little secret

DON JUAN

Why?

THE DEVIL

Because I thought his precious chosen creatures could not find out the truth and keep on living, I admit I misjudged you.

DON JUAN

Well, you were less subtle when you were a snake. The worm's not the only thing I discovered after biting that apple. First there was Eve; Lilith came second, and between them was begat, thirdly, the clothing industry. Thanks to that unholy trinity, I've given up one pallid Paradise, but in its place I've entered, night after night, a thousand blissful gardens. *(Calls.)* Sganarelle!

(SGANARELLE enters.)

SGANARELLE

Sir?

DON JUAN

Bring me my catalog.

(SGANARELLE sees THE DEVIL and stiffens.)

Yes, yes, it's just who you think it is. My list!

(Crossing himself, SGA-NARELLE gladly exits. He immediately returns with a sheaf of papers, which he gives to Don Juan.)

SGANARELLE (murmurs in DON JUAN'S ear)

Is there anyone I should tell not to expect you tonight?

DON JUAN

No, you could never get to all of them in time. And besides, I have an excellent chance of survival. *(He removes a ring from his hand.)* But just in case I don't, here's the ruby I promised you.

(SGANARELLE pounces on the ring and exits.)

THE DEVIL (raising his wineglass)

Now there's devotion for you. A toast to your poverty, Don Juan.

DON JUAN

What! Look around you. Are these the appurtenances of squalor?

THE DEVIL

I'm referring to your dearth of friends.

DON JUAN

I didn't seek the comradeship of lesser men.

THE DEVIL

What about family?

DON JUAN *(uncomfortably)*

I had the customary complement of parents.

THE DEVIL

You leave nothing behind you.

DON JUAN *(showing his list)*

False. Here's my legacy.

THE DEVIL

A catalog of women's names?

DON JUAN

I said I would debauch a thousand virtuous women, and here you see I bettered that by three.

THE DEVIL

You sacrificed eternal grace for ephemeral pleasure?

DON JUAN

I eternally found pleasure in feminine grace.

THE DEVIL *(examining the list)*

Statistically, it's positively astonishing.

DON JUAN

What is?

THE DEVIL

The number of times you did the deed—*(DON JUAN smiles.)* —and yet you leave behind no son to mourn your death.

(DON JUAN frowns.)

DON JUAN

I'm glad. His reputation might have vitiated mine.

THE DEVIL

You're satisfied with renown?

DON JUAN

I am. The world envies me. I'm the hero of all great novels, protagonist of the most successful plays. What daring kiss is not stolen in my name? What secret and forbidden act is not dedicate to my enduring spirit? Each man grieves because he's but a counterfeit Don Juan. *(He points to his list.)* This grand catalog's my testament to all that I possessed.

THE DEVIL *(rising from the table)*

Possessed? Now there's an interesting word. I have many "spiritual" possessions, but what can you possibly own? This scrap of paper with faded names upon it?

(He reads from the list.)

"Babette . . . Sylvette . . ." Peut-etre. Possession, then, is nothing more than carnal knowledge?

DON JUAN

You must emphasize the word "knowledge." Knowing means far more than merely having.

THE DEVIL

Now let's see whether I understand you, Don Juan. Because you've had—and known—these thousand and three women, you claim you've also possessed them?

DON JUAN

That's the glory that Hell can never diminish. I clasped their unclad bodies and penetrated their naked spirits.

THE DEVIL

All thousand and three?

DON JUAN

Each had her own secret.

THE DEVIL

Which you remember?

DON JUAN

Yes.

THE DEVIL

Then why do you need this list?

DON JUAN

I don't.

THE DEVIL

I'm unconvinced.

DON JUAN

I'll prove it to you.

> (DON JUAN *takes the list from*
> THE DEVIL *and begins to tear*
> *it to bits.* THE DEVIL *fetches*
> *the hat he wore as the* MARI-
> ONETTE MASTER *and holds*
> *it upside down.* DON JUAN
> *shreds his catalog and puts the*
> *tattered bits inside the hat.)*

Observe that each was a virtuous lady. I promised you that.

THE DEVIL

Don't stop till there's a thousand and three pieces.

DON JUAN *(still ripping his list)*

I avoided loose women because, like you, Lucifer, I take delight in
tarnishing the innocent; their tardy expressions of remorse delight Don
Juan. *(He drops the last scraps into the hat.)* There, that's the lot . . . one
thousand and three names . . . will you test me now?

THE DEVIL

I will.

> (THE DEVIL *takes the hat to*
> *the balcony and makes a mystic*

pass over it. A burst of flame. The hat is empty.)

DON JUAN

Bravo, puppeteer! I see you're also a magician.

THE DEVIL

Yes, but the trick's just beginning,

(He sweeps his arm out over the balcony.)

Abracadabra!

(A soft white light begins to glow beneath the balcony.)

DON JUAN

Where's that light coming from?

THE DEVIL

Look and see.

(DON JUAN joins THE DEVIL at the balcony.)

DON JUAN

A thousand gondolas on the lagoon?

THE DEVIL

A thousand and three.

DON JUAN

Who rides inside?

THE DEVIL

The spirit of every woman you say that you possessed. I've brought them back to life.

DON JUAN *(watches them, fascinated)*

They're disembarking.

(The light grows brighter.)

THE DEVIL

And now?

DON JUAN

The ghosts are coming up the stairs. Each one wears a mask.

> *(*THE DEVIL *gestures dramatically. The white light explodes into dazzling brilliance arid then dwindles into a spotlight highlighting the puppet theatre.)*

What happened?

THE DEVIL *(putting on the hat)*

That was the end of the trick. Now I'm master of marionettes once more. *(He calls)* Begin the show!

> *(A masked ghost appears upon the puppet stage.)*

THE GHOST

Don Juan, I bid you a good evening.

DON JUAN *(approaching her)*

Lovely phantom, would you dine with me? And let me lift the veil that sheathes your mysteries?

> *(He reaches for her mask.)*

THE DEVIL

Hands off.

> *(*DON JUAN *looks at him, startled.)*

She may only make one revelation to you, Don Juan.

DON JUAN

And that is?

THE DEVIL

The deepest secret of her soul. If you can hear it and then reveal her name, I'll permit her to lower her mask.

DON JUAN

So that's your test? *(Smiling)* I expected worse. *(Addressing her)* Let's hear your secret, then.

THE GHOST

I always had—

> *(She whispers the rest directly into* DON JUAN*'S ear.)*

DON JUAN

You suffered deep regrets each time you made love, and yet you could not stop yourself?

> *(She turns away, ashamed.* DON JUAN *tries to take her hand.)*

Don't be distressed, it's such a common—

THE DEVIL *(interrupting)*

Touch her spirit, not her flesh!

DON JUAN

Well, you started me with an easy riddle. *(He speaks ardently to her.)* This can only be my passionate, yet remorseful . . . Lucette.

THE GHOST

I always loved the way you spoke my name—

DON JUAN *(to THE DEVIL)*

You see? Lucette.

THE GHOST

—but when I hear you murmur "Lucette" like that, it practically convinces me that's who I am.

DON JUAN

What? You're not Lucette?

THE GHOST

No.

> *(She disappears from the puppet stage. A SECOND GHOST immediately takes her place.)*

SECOND GHOST

What about me?

DON JUAN *(reaching for her hand)*

Your voice sounds familiar, I—

THE DEVIL

No touching!

DON JUAN

Well, then, tell me your secret.

> *(She murmurs to him.)*

Ah, there's a day I'll never forget! Eluding your mother and her mangy poodle in the crowd . . . the fireworks . . .

SECOND GHOST

I did behave badly.

DON JUAN

Not at all . You performed magnificently . . . Suzette . . .

SECOND GHOST

That's not my name.

> *(She leaves the puppet stage.)*

DON JUAN

Impossible! The circumstances of our tryst—

THE DEVIL *(interrupting)*

—are thoroughly banal.

DON JUAN *(rallying with a laugh)*

You're right. So many damsels have slipped away with me from their mothers and their mutts, it's easy to mix them up.

THIRD GHOST *(appears on puppet stage)*

Will you confuse me, too?

> *(She whispers to* DON JUAN.*)*

DON JUAN

Oh, you always expected too much. You should have paid less attention to the way you looked and more to how you felt . . . your far-too-serene Highness.

THIRD GHOST

Wrong again.

> *(She leaves. A fourth ghost instantly takes her place.)*

FOURTH GHOST *(after whispering to him)*

Well?

DON JUAN *(his confidence waning)*

Yvette?

FOURTH GHOST

No.

DON JUAN

Colette?

FOURTH GHOST

No.

DON JUAN *(snaps fingers)*

I have it! You are the daughter of the innkeeper.

FOURTH GHOST

No.

(She leaves and is immediately replaced by another.)

FIFTH GHOST

Who am I, Don Juan?

(She whispers her secret.)

DON JUAN

I had you after the bullfight . . . Conchette . . . ?

FIFTH GHOST

No.

(She leaves. Another is already whispering to DON JUAN.*)*

DON JUAN *(with great relief)*

Your jealousy betrays you, at least. Your daughter was my cousin Tristette. First I had her, and then you, my own Aunt Rivette.

SIXTH GHOST

No.

DON JUAN *(in a rage)*

Liar!

*(*DON JUAN *lunges at her, but she disappears.)*

THE DEVIL

Here, now, don't mistreat my property!

DON JUAN

Every one of them is lying to me.

(The sound of the women laughing.)

THE DEVIL

Lying? Not so. They're laughing.

DON JUAN

I've often heard women's laughter, but never before like this.

THE DEVIL

How could you? This is the joke that women only share in private.

DON JUAN

What joke is that?

THE DEVIL

Man. They titter at posturing peacocks who strut and call themselves possessors.

DON JUAN

Bid them be silent! Like you, I won't be mocked.

> (THE DEVIL *claps. The laughter ceases.*)

You won't crush my spirit quite so easily, Lucifer. You see I've regained my customary calm? Forget my past mistakes. I'm going to start all over again.

THE DEVIL *(Sighs)*

Ah, well, the night's still young.

> (*Sitting down, he pours himself more wine and ignores* DON JUAN.)
>
> (*The whispering ghosts appear and disappear in rapid succession.*)

DON JUAN

All right, let's begin once more.

> (*Listens to a ghost's secret*)

Annette . . . ?

SEVENTH GHOST

No.

DON JUAN *(hears another secret)*

Arlette . . . ?

EIGHTH GHOST

No.

DON JUAN *(hears another)*

Aurette . . . ?

NINTH GHOST

(As the lights fade, two ghosts and then a third ring round DON JUAN and whisper.)

DON JUAN

Babette . . . ? Barbette . . . ? Bibette . . . ?

THE GHOSTS

No . . . No . . . No . . .

(The lights fade out.)

SCENE TWO

The same, shortly before dawn. DON JUAN, holding the lit candelabra, is studying THE DEVIL, who seems to be asleep. DON JUAN stealthily approaches the latest GHOST in the puppet theatre.

DON JUAN *(sotto voce)*

Quickly now, while the Devil's asleep, assist me. For the sake of the passion we once shared, will you remove your mask?

GHOST

Yes.

> *(She takes it off, but there is another mask underneath it.)*

DON JUAN

A second mask? Will you take that one off, too?

GHOST

I will.

> *(She does, but beneath it is a third mask.)*

DON JUAN

How many are you wearing?

THE DEVIL

More than anyone can count. In life, she hid behind so many masks that she ended up obliterating her own face.

> *(DON JUAN sets down the candelabra. The GHOST exits.)*

DON JUAN *(disgusted)*

It's useless. I thought I knew my lovers, but it seems they're all strangers to me.

THE DEVIL *(rising)*

You thought you were on intimate terms with their souls, so by your own admission, you die possessing nothing.

DON JUAN

Not so fast. The spirit is sadly mutable. It's true I do not know them now, but when they lay with me, I knew everything about them.

THE DEVIL *(sits back down)*

Indeed?

> *(*THE DEVIL *claps. Three ghosts appear on the puppet stage.)*

Is what he says the truth?

> *(The ghosts titter their private laugh.)*

THE THREE GHOSTS *(together)*

Since when do men seek truth?

THE MIDDLE GHOST

They see us through a mist of their own imagining.

THE THREE GHOSTS *(together)*

We lie to them accordingly.

THE GHOST ON THE LEFT *(stage right)*

Don Juan thought me intelligent, so I boned up on the classics and dazzled him with warmed-over Petrarch.

THE GHOST ON THE RIGHT *(stage left)*

Don Juan called me prudish, so I pretended to be shocked when he did things to me that I wanted him to.

THE MIDDLE GHOST

Don Juan had a whim to destroy my supposedly happy home, therefore I fawned like a bride over my odious husband.

THE GHOSTS ON THE LEFT AND RIGHT *(together)*

Women know how to give men what they think they want—

THE THREE GHOSTS *(together)*

The Eternal Feminine!

THE GHOST ON THE RIGHT

A notion so silly that only a man could have thought it up.

THE DEVIL *(rising)*

Now what do you think of your thousand and three paramours, Don Juan?

DON JUAN

Odious hypocrites!

THE DEVIL

And now it's time to take you to Hell.

DON JUAN

Not yet. I'm still buoyant.

THE DEVIL

Your reason?

DON JUAN

I am an offshoot of the Conquistadores. My forefathers subdued the Indian continent, but they never understood the nature of the Indians.

THE DEVIL

Oho, so that's your tack. You're telling me that possession is not knowledge after all, but of a different nature?

DON JUAN

Yes.

THE DEVIL

What is it, then? Instruct me.

DON JUAN

Possession is equivalent to domination. I'm proud because my lust overrode their virtue.

THE DEVIL *(turns to the ghosts)*

Is what he says the truth? When did you first experience desire for Don Juan?

THE GHOST ON THE RIGHT

The very moment I saw him.

THE GHOST ON THE LEFT

The instant that I saw him.

THE MIDDLE GHOST

The first time I heard about him.

DON JUAN

But it was I who did the seducing!

THE THREE GHOSTS *(together)*

At our bidding.

DON JUAN

Impossible. How?

THE GHOST ON THE LEFT

The way I looked down.

THE GHOST ON THE RIGHT

The way I looked up.

THE THREE GHOSTS *(together)*

The way we walked.

THE MIDDLE GHOST

The way I laughed.

THE THREE GHOSTS *(together)*

The way we breathed.

DON JUAN

But some of you were virgins.

THE DEVIL

They were less skilled.

DON JUAN

And some of you were noblewomen.

THE DEVIL

They were better at it.

THE THREE GHOSTS *(together)*

Men have prostitutes. We had Don Juan.

THE DEVIL

You thought you were uppermost in their hearts, but I had them long before you did.

> *(He prepares to seize* DON JUAN.*)*

And now—

DON JUAN

Keep your claws to yourself, you haven't humbled me yet.

THE DEVIL

What? Still an ounce of pride remaining? In what?

DON JUAN

In being chosen.

THE DEVIL

You can't be serious!

DON JUAN

I am. *(He murmurs to himself)* I must be.

THE DEVIL

You're proud because a thousand and three strangers selected you?

DON JUAN *(revising his answer)*

Not just that. Because I gave them pleasure.

THE DEVIL *(to the ghosts)*

Is what he says—

(He stops, smiles sardonically and offers his hat to DON JUAN.)

Would you like to play the puppeteer this time?

DON JUAN *(declining the hat)*

No.

THE DEVIL

Has Don Juan's vaunted courage finally deserted him?

DON JUAN

No!

THE DEVIL

Then ask your lovers what delighted them about you.

(DON JUAN reluctantly turns to the women.)

DON JUAN

Well?

THE MIDDLE GHOST

I liked the way you smell.

DON JUAN

The scent of brimstone?

THE MIDDLE GHOST *(titters)*

No, silly! A mixture of perfume and tobacco.

DON JUAN *(to the ghost on the left)*

What about you?

THE GHOST ON THE LEFT

I liked the way you dress.

DON JUAN

That's all?

THE GHOST ON THE LEFT

For me it was.

DON JUAN *(to the remaining ghost)*

And you?

THE GHOST ON THE RIGHT

I enjoyed the challenge.

DON JUAN

Can't you be more specific?

THE GHOST ON THE RIGHT

It excited me to think I might sleep with a man who'd had so many other women.

DON JUAN *(to THE DEVIL)*

This is an answer I like.

THE DEVIL *(to her)*

And was he what you thought he'd be?

THE GHOST ON THE RIGHT

Alas, no. When I found out how easy it was to have him, I realized he wasn't a real challenge, after all.

> *(DON JUAN clasps the back of a chair to steady himself.)*

THE DEVIL *(after a pause)*

I think you're done now, aren't you?

> *(DON JUAN stares bleakly at THE DEVIL, then with an heroic effort, he straightens and defiantly crosses his arms.)*

What? Courageous still?

DON JUAN *(to the women)*

I am a giant, yet you belittle me. Why? Because although you may have had me at your will, it was I who walked out on every one of you. And so I scorn your malicious intent.

THE MIDDLE GHOST

You didn't walk out on us.

THE GHOST ON THE LEFT

You ran away from us.

DON JUAN

Nonsense. Why would I?

THE GHOST ON THE LEFT

Because you were afraid.

DON JUAN

Don Juan afraid? Ridiculous! Afraid of what?

THE GHOST ON THE LEFT

Of heartbreak.

THE GHOST ON THE RIGHT

Of tenderness.

THE THREE GHOSTS *(together)*

Of love.

DON JUAN *(an anguished cry)*

Aaahhh!

> *(He buries his head in his hands.)*

THE DEVIL

Twist yourself inside out, Don Juan, Try to find something else to be proud of in your helter-skelter life.

> *(Desperately rallying, DON JUAN straightens.)*

Out of agony comes strength?

DON JUAN

De profundis. You ought to know.

THE DEVIL

Touché. What straw are you grasping at this time?

DON JUAN

I'm the lover who always won out over other lovers. I never wished to be any other man.

THE DEVIL *(tauntingly)*

Not even your brother Punch?

DON JUAN

I've finally defeated you, Lucifer. There isn't a man you could mention whose name would fill me with envy.

THE DEVIL *(turning to the women)*

You hear the challenge. Is what he says the truth?

THE GHOST ON THE LEFT

What about Romeo?

THE GHOST ON THE RIGHT

Or Cyrano?

THE MIDDLE GHOST

Or Lancelot?

THE GHOST ON THE LEFT

Those are the lovers we longed for.

THE GHOST ON THE RIGHT

But being pragmatic, we settled for you.

DON JUAN

Shut up!

THE GHOST ON THE LEFT

Romeo.

THE DEVIL

Try to better his poetry.

THE MIDDLE GHOST

Lancelot.

THE DEVIL

Try to better his courage.

THE GHOST ON THE RIGHT

Cyrano.

THE DEVIL

I'd like to see you slay him in a duel!

> (DON JUAN *wildly shakes his fists at the women.)*

DON JUAN

I made all of you suffer!

THE MIDDLE GHOST

And never understood why.

DON JUAN

Who cares? I ravished, but I did not deign to delve. Shall I sip poison like adolescent Romeo? Or stand behind the scenes like Cyrano and prompt my rival as he woos? Or go on needless quests for spurious grails? No, I am Don Juan the Blasphemer! I take what woman I want and stand unmoved while she sheds bitter tears. There's my pride!

> (THE DEVIL *hands* DON JUAN *an empty wineglass.)*

THE DEVIL

Let's take up a collection, shall we?

DON JUAN

Of what?

THE DEVIL

Of tears these women shed for you. Give them the goblet.

> *(DON JUAN unwillingly takes the wineglass to the women. They accept it from him and each brings it to her eyes and pretends to weep in it.)*

THE GHOST ON THE LEFT

Boo-hoo!

THE MIDDLE GHOST

Boo-hoo!

THE GHOST ON THE RIGHT

Boo-hoo!

> *(Then, furtively, she spits in the cup.)*

THE DEVIL

Now take the cup to your sisters.

> *(The women exit.)*

A thousand sufferers to go, Don Juan.

> *(The lights fade.)*

SCENE THREE

The same. Early morning THE DEVIL *is drawing a black velvet curtain across the rear of the room while* DON JUAN *stands by, admiring the filled goblet that he holds.*

THE DEVIL *(letting go of the curtain)*
There, that's better. Daylight spoils a spectre's complexion. Let's see the tears, Don Juan.

DON JUAN *(handing him the cup)*
You see how much they wept for me? The goblet is brimming over. Put me in Hell's hottest compartment and these cool crystal drops will still refresh me. I wonder that you dare come near them, Lucifer. I'd heard they're almost as dangerous to you as holy water.

THE DEVIL
You heard right. True tears burn me. But let's examine these.

> *(*THE DEVIL *flings the cup so that the tears spatter against the velvet curtain. They remain there, shimmering like tiny stars.* THE DEVIL *produces a magnifying glass and inspects the tears.)*

False. False. False. False. False.

DON JUAN
They can't all be false!

THE DEVIL
No? *(He studies more tears.)* False. False. False. False, False.

DON JUAN *(pointing to one of them)*
What about this one?

THE DEVIL
She was angry because she didn't get a birthday present she wanted. She let you borrow that tear.

DON JUAN *(points to another)*
What about this one?

THE DEVIL
She happened to prick her finger just before you arrived.

DON JUAN
What about this huge teardrop?

THE DEVIL *(laughs)*
That spiteful lady spat into your cup.

DON JUAN
What about the small clear ones? What are they?

THE DEVIL
Secret tears.

DON JUAN
Then they must count!

> *(THE DEVIL touches a few.)*

THE DEVIL
No, I can touch them. You weren't the secret behind them.

DON JUAN
Father of Lies, you're lying to me!

THE DEVIL
You think so? Watch.
> *(He runs his talons over the curtain, touching tear after tear after tear.)*

False. False. False. False. Fal—
> *(He suddenly cries out in pain.)*

OWWW!!!

DON JUAN *(joyous)*
You found a real tear!

THE DEVIL *(sourly, sucking his claw)*

Obviously.

DON JUAN

Whose?

A WOMAN'S VOICE

It's my tear.

DON JUAN

Come show yourself to me.

THE VOICE

May I?

THE DEVIL *(grumpily)*

Oh, go ahead.

> *(A masked spirit clad in delicate silver-white enters the room. DON JUAN approaches her.)*

DON JUAN

Which one of my lovers were you?

THE SILVER SPIRIT

One who died young. Like the tear I shed for you, pity made me fall.

DON JUAN

Pity because I made you a fallen woman?

THE SILVER SPIRIT

No. Pity for your pain.

DON JUAN

And what was that?

THE SILVER SPIRIT

And what is that? The agony I sense behind your pride. The little boy who lurks inside the man and cries for arms to comfort him.

DON JUAN

Ah, tell me your name, sweet spirit

(She whispers it to him.)

I don't recognize it

THE SILVER SPIRIT *(reaching for her mask)*

Then see me plain!

THE DEVIL

No!

(But she strips it away and shows DON JUAN *her face. A tense moment and then* DON JUAN *speaks.)*

DON JUAN

I don't remember you. When did we meet? In what place? If only I had my list . . .

THE DEVIL *(his composure has returned)*

I've got a copy.

(He produces a duplicate of the list from a pocket and hands it to DON JUAN.*)*

DON JUAN *(riffling feverishly)*

Darlette . . . Evalette . . . Friedette . . . Why can't I find her? It's all the fault of that villainous Sganarelle!

THE DEVIL

No, Don Juan, this is the one name you neglected to mention to him. Cheer up. You wanted to stop at an even number. Now will you admit I've won?

DON JUAN

Shall I be sad because I slept with one thousand and three false women and missed true love only once?

(THE SILVER SPIRIT dons her mask and runs to the puppet stage where the other ghosts emerge and join her. They all are dressed identically to THE SILVER SPIRIT.)

THE SILVER SPIRIT

Only once?

(She runs behind the other ghosts.)

DON JUAN

Where are you?

THE SILVER SPIRIT

Only once?

(She runs to the end of the line.)

DON JUAN

Take off your mask. I can't tell which one you are.

THE SILVER SPIRIT

That's your sorrow. You could have found true love like mine in any one of your women. Poor Don Juan . . .

THE THREE GHOSTS *(together)*

In any one of us you might have found true love . . . poor Don Juan . . .

(THE THREE GHOSTS hold out their arms to DON JUAN. He starts towards them.)

THE DEVIL

Stop this sudden show of tenderness!

(THE THREE GHOSTS turn their backs on DON JUAN.)

If I hadn't been here, goodness might have triumphed after all.

DON JUAN *(to THE SILVER SPIRIT)*

I'm sorry I did not fall in love with you.

THE SILVER SPIRIT

It's still not too late.

DON JUAN

I don't know how.

THE SILVER SPIRIT

It isn't hard, I'll show you.

THE DEVIL *(in consternation)*

Double damn! If she really teaches him, I'll lose!

THE SILVER SPIRIT *(removing her mask)*

Look into my eyes and say you long to hold me.

DON JUAN *(looking into her eyes)*

I long to hold you.

THE SILVER SPIRIT

Clasp me close and tell me that you give yourself to me in the spirit of true love.

DON JUAN *(embracing her)*

I give myself to you in the spirit of true love.

THE DEVIL

What a puppet you make, Don Juan. She pulls your strings and you respond.

DON JUAN

What do you expect? I'm new at this game.

(He speaks to THE SILVER SPIRIT.*)*

From now on, I dedicate my heart to you alone.

*(THE DEVIL gestures. THE
THREE GHOSTS turn around
and take off their masks.)*

THE THREE GHOSTS *(together)*

To her alone?

(They laugh maliciously.)

DON JUAN *(staring at them)*

At last! So that's what you look like.

THE SILVER SPIRIT

Remember how they lied to you.

DON JUAN

I do. There's the fascination.

THE THREE GHOSTS *(coquettishly)*

Ahhh?

DON JUAN

The last time around I didn't really know you. So, in effect, you're one thousand and three brand-new challenges.

THE THREE GHOSTS *(appreciatively)*

Ahhh!

THE SILVER SPIRIT *(despairingly)*

Ahhh. Poor Don Juan.

DON JUAN *(to her)*

Oh, go away. You're becoming a bore. True love, indeed! The only thing I've ever loved is the quest. Women are but implements I use to overleap myself. One does not fall in love with tools.

*(THE THREE GHOSTS exit in-
dignantly, THE SILVER SPIR-
IT stays.)*

THE DEVIL

Snatching at gambits even in the endgame, eh? What does it mean, Don Juan, to overleap the Self?

DON JUAN

To rest in restless ecstasy. Women were merely the means.

THE DEVIL

I see, You employed them like a painter wields his palette?

DON JUAN

Yes.

THE DEVIL

But towards what end?

DON JUAN *(uncomfortably)*

What do you mean?

THE DEVIL

Did they inspire you to fashion great works of art to be remembered by? Perhaps another *La Gioconda*? Or a new Botticellian Venus? Did you compose romantic sonnets? Or symphonies of fire and color and force?

DON JUAN *(in real anguish)*

Stop it!

THE DEVIL

At last you mourn yourself in earnest.

> (THE SILVER SPIRIT *flies to the side of* DON JUAN.)

THE SILVER SPIRIT *(cradling his head)*

Here's the sorrow I shed tears for. Tell me.

DON JUAN *(bleakly)*

I dallied with exquisite women, but never created anything exquisite myself. I warred with mankind, but where are the battle hymns I might have penned? You shed love's tear for me, but I have no heart to break.

The only thing I did was make a list.

(He slowly rises and faces THE
DEVIL.)

You've won, Lucifer, I have no torch to pass and so I myself must
burn. But still I will not beg for mercy. Call me any name you want: Don
Wan, Don Joo-ann, Don Giovanni, John Tanner or Mister Jack, I'm still
the Blasphemer of Seville.

THE DEVIL
A final scrap of pride just because you exist. Well, you forgot one
name. Still spitting out apples, Adam?

DON JUAN
Yes. But on the final day, we'll see. My will may yet outlast the
apple, worm and tree.

THE DEVIL *(sneers)*
Perhaps. But on your final night, did you make the Devil suffer?

DON JUAN
I did.

THE DEVIL
What? How?

DON JUAN
By reminding you how painful it is not to be a creator.

*(*THE DEVIL *reels as if struck.)*

The damned cannot create. That's the true nature of Hell, isn't it?

THE DEVIL *(a hoarse whisper)*
Yes.

DON JUAN
Does that make you pity the damned?

THE DEVIL *(viciously)*

No . . . I hate myself in them!

(He seizes DON JUAN *and drags him toward the puppet stage.)*

Now come and join their company.

*(*THE SILVER SPIRIT *steps in the path of* THE DEVIL.*)*

THE SILVER SPIRIT

Stop! It's not too late, Don Juan.

DON JUAN

You're wrong. I'm ready for Hell.

THE SILVER SPIRIT

As long as the tear I shed for you is still damp, there's time to save yourself. Love me!

DON JUAN

Haven't you heard? The Devil and I are much alike. He trots on cloven hooves. I wear them on my brow to signify I browsed through life, a goatish satyr. Goatishly, I swallowed everything I could and left nothing growing where I passed. Let me burn!

THE DEVIL

Step aside, You cannot save him.

THE SILVER SPIRIT *(defiantly)*

My tear is still moist!

(To DON JUAN, *with desperate intensity)*

All your life you set yourself at odds with yourself. Let me love you and I'll teach you how to love yourself.

DON JUAN

Stop whining, woman! I spurn salvation, whether it's yours or God's. I yearn for Hell and the company of Caligula and Nero and all my fellow monsters.

> (THE SILVER SPIRIT *shrinks into the background.* THE DEVIL *shoves* DON JUAN *to the edge of the puppet theatre.* PUNCH *pops up onstage.)*

PUNCH

Don Juan, at last! Hurrah!

DON JUAN *(to THE DEVIL)*

See here, where are you taking me?

THE DEVIL

Into your Attic temple.

DON JUAN

Is it actually the gate to the fiery inferno?

THE DEVIL

One of them. A sort of Hell in miniature.

PUNCH *(ringing his bell)*

Brother degenerate, hurrah!

> (THE THREE GHOSTS *enter and take chairs facing the puppet stage. They all sit immodestly.)*

DON JUAN *(horrified)*

Not the puppet stage itself?

THE DEVIL

Indeed, yes.

(He attaches strings to DON JUAN.*)*

You'll be one of my most popular marionettes, forever strutting your peacock bravado before a canvas backcloth.

(He pushes him onstage.)

DON JUAN
But I deserve a hero's punishment! Take me down to Hell!

(The three ghosts titter.)

THE DEVIL
Hell is where I will it. Some men's souls are locked inside their statues. Yours makes a far better puppet.

DON JUAN
But I'm the son of the conquering Conquistadores!

*(*THE THREE GHOSTS *laugh.)*

I demand everlasting flames!

THE DEVIL
Too bad. I damn you to everlasting theatre.

*(*DON JUAN *screams.)*

PUNCH
Hsst, brother . . . !

DON JUAN *(distracted by PUNCH)*
Eh? What?

PUNCH *(murmurs in DON JUAN'S ear)*
From here, you can look up their skirts.

DON JUAN *(sees that it is true)*
Well, old serpent, if this is the apple you'd have me bite, why not? The marble statue's immobile, but the marionette knows how to move . . . and mock.

PUNCH

Hurrah! A new script!

THE DEVIL

We'll see. Don't keep your audience waiting, Don Juan-n-n-n-ette.

(He claps his hands.)

DON JUAN *(sings)*

I'm the marionette, Don Juan.
I love ladies with élan,
And I always heat their beds.

(THE THREE GHOSTS titter, PUNCH and DON JUAN put their arms around one another, DON JUAN keeps ducking his head to see up the women's skirts.)

DON JUAN (sings)

I'm the marionette, Don Juan.
I love ladies with élan,
And I always heat their beds.

PUNCH (sings)

I'm the famous puppet, Punch.
I love ladies by the bunch.
But I always beat their heads

(THE SILVER SPIRIT looks at the velvet curtain.)

THE SILVER SPIRIT *(mournfully)*

Alas, my teardrop has dried up and gone away. It never will return.

(Curtain)

MISTER JACK — FOR BETTER OR FOR WORSE

CHARACTERS

LEO

MR. JACK

DANA, *Leo's wife*

KATHLEEN

VIOLETTA, *Kathleen's sister*

NOTE:

KATHLEEN *and* VIOLETTA *are played by the same actor.*

The three women's hair colors and styles should be different.

The author is indebted to the Don Juan plays of Tirso de Molina, Molière, Edmond Rostand and Bernard Shaw, as well as Lorenzo da Ponte's libretto for Mozart. The 1st scene is loosely patterned on Alfred Sutro's one-act play *The Man in the Stalls.*

SETTING AND TIME SYNOPSIS

ACT ONE

SCENE 1: Leo's home. Early evening.
SCENE 2: The same. Later that night.
SCENE 3: The same. A few weeks later.
SCENE 4: This theatre.
SCENE 5: Leo's home. Later.

ACT TWO

SCENE 1: Leo's home.
SCENE 2: This theatre. Several months later.
SCENE 3: Leo's home. Later that night.

BEFORE THE SHOW BEGINS

5 x 8 cards (blue for men, pink for women) should be distributed and collected. Each card contains the following printed information —

- -

MR. JACK, DIRECT DESCENDANT OF DON JUAN TEN-ORIO AND THE WORLD'S GREATEST LIVING LOVER, WILL ANSWER YOUR QUESTIONS ABOUT LOVE AND INTIMACY.

Your Question?

_____

_____

_____

- -

ACT ONE

SCENE ONE

> LEO's *living room; early eve-*
> *ning. Three exits: outside, up-*
> *stairs, and a wing where* MR.
> JACK *and* KATHLEEN *have*
> *rooms.* MR. JACK *is seated at*
> *a table sipping scotch and shuf-*
> *fling cards.* LEO *is putting on*
> *jacket and tie at a mirror.*

LEO

Oh God, another night at the theatuh! *(Indicates MR. J)* Look at him, sitting on his ass. Mr. Jack, the World's Greatest Lover! Now he just lays — around the house.

MR. JACK

Leo, don't be crude.

LEO

My house.

MR. JACK

You got rich peddling me in public. My sins swung your mortgage.

LEO

(Knotting his tie) What've you done for me lately?

MR. JACK

The book you wrote about me got you your job.

LEO

The worst job in the world.

MR. JACK

The easiest. You get to see all the new plays for free.

LEO

Which is what they're worth.

MR. JACK

You put that in the column you write, and you get paid for it.

LEO

Not enough for being bored night after night.

MR. JACK

Boredom? Try spending the night teaching your wife how to play bridge.

LEO

Tell her that, I dare you. She's the reason you're still here.

MR. JACK

I know. Dana pities me.

> *NOTE:* MR. JACK *always says her name correctly: DAH-NAH.* LEO *says DAY-NAH.*

LEO

Well, you're pitiable. When's the last time you got it up?

MR. JACK

When's the last time I wanted to?

LEO

You didn't use to be so choosy.

MR. JACK

We all change. Remember your first wife?

LEO

I try not to. That bitch slept with anything: men, women, dogs, hair brushes. *(Suddenly)* Did *you* do her? *(No reply.)* Of course you did. You're Mr. Jack.

MR. JACK

Are you upset?

LEO

I would be if it were Dana, but — no.

DANA *(entering)*

Leo, you're going to be late. Ahh, that knot! Let me fix it. *(She begins to redo his tie.)*

MR. JACK

So what are you seeing tonight?

LEO

Comedy, drama, half the time I can't tell which. This one's called *Bosom Buddies.*

MR. JACK

What's it about?

LEO

About two hours too long. Hey, you're choking me!

DANA

I'm sick of that stupid joke.

LEO

Act One: John nails Bob's wife. Act Two: John feels SO guilty, he confesses and Bob beats the shit out of him. Christ, I worked for you, what, twenty years, Mr. J.? Nobody ever stood up to you like that. You would have bust their balls!

MR. JACK

(Deals bridge hands) If you must dwell on the past, why must it always be *my* past?

DANA

Better than his own.

LEO

Working for you, I learned most husbands don't act like The Terminator.

DANA

So if I was unfaithful, you wouldn't mind? Good to know.

LEO

I'm not talking about me. I'm talking about the average husband.

DANA

(Sotto voce) That does leave you out.

MR. JACK

So Mrs. Average sleeps with her hubby's best friend. What *does* Mr. Average do?

LEO

Probably says, *I'm* supposed to sleep with her. What's your excuse?

MR. JACK

(Sighs) You always had a gift for noble sentiment.

DANA

Leo, it's twenty-five of.

LEO

Yeah. Have a good game, you two. I'll grab a cab.

> *He exits. They wait for the slam*
> *of the door.*

MR. JACK

Poor Leo. *(Turns over dummy hand)* Never satisfied.

DANA

How *can* he be, living in your shadow?

MR. JACK

My shadow? That's all that's left. Law suits wiped me out. One of the many reasons Leo disapproves of the life I led.

DANA

Because he didn't lead it himself. Enough talk about Leo. Enough talk.

> *She takes his hand and presses it*
> *to her breast.*

MR. JACK

Weren't you uncomfortable when he talked about cheating?

DANA

It excited me. How you feel excites me. (*Nips him*) Your taste. The way you smell.

MR. JACK

I'm supposed to be teaching you bridge.

DANA

(*Leans over to kiss him*) Not tonight, lover . . .

MR. JACK

(*Avoids her lips*) Better not. Kathleen might walk in on us.

DANA

It's her day off. She's been out for hours.

> *Rising, he goes to pour himself a drink.*

MR. JACK

She might come back any second then.

DANA

She won't. She's with her guy.

MR. JACK

How do you know that?

DANA

I recognize the symptoms.

MR. JACK

You have undiscovered talents. What symptoms?

DANA

What is this, a talk show? If you've got to exercise your tongue —

MR. JACK

Dana, don't be crude.

DANA

Sorry. Bad habit I got into. Subtlety's wasted on Leo.

MR. JACK

I've got to tell you something. It's important.

DANA

(A short frustrated silence) All right, spit it out.

MR. JACK

I'm going to get married.

DANA

(After a beat) I'm waiting for the punch-line.

MR. JACK

It's not a joke.

DANA

Married? *(Begins to laugh)* YOU?

MR. JACK

(To audience) Listen to that! All my life, I've been raked over the coals. I try to change, to become respectable — *this* is the reaction I get!

DANA

Since when have you ever cared about respectability?

MR. JACK

Since I started growing old.

DANA

Oh, that's what this is about? Midlife crisis?

MR. JACK

I need to find myself. I'm just not sure there's anything worth finding.

DANA

Scratch crisis. Full-blown existential *angst.*

MR. JACK

I'm just . . . lonely.

DANA

That's silly. You live here with me and Leo.

MR. JACK

Which is a big part of the problem. I'm sponging off a man who used to work for me. And if that's not bad enough, look what we're doing to him.

DANA

A conscience? *You?!* For God's sake!

MR. JACK

Not for God's sake, not for Lucifer's. I'm ashamed of myself.

DANA

Not enough to stay out of my bed.

MR. JACK

You wanted me.

DANA

And you got nothing out of it? *(Pause)* And you got *nothing* out of it?

MR. JACK

Do you really want me to answer that?

DANA

(After a long dangerous silence) Who is she?

MR. JACK

Never mind.

DANA

Oh, in other words, I know her.

MR. JACK

Let it go, Dana.

DANA

Only who do you know besides me? You never leave the house! *(In sudden horror)* Oh, my God, not — KATHLEEN?!

MR. JACK

Kathleen.

DANA

She's twenty-fucking years younger.

MR. JACK

The hyperbole of spite. That's fifteen years.

DANA

She's just learning things you threw out before she was born!

MR. JACK

Maybe that's part of her charm.

DANA

You made love to her in my house!

MR. JACK

No, I have not. But you and I made love under Leo's roof.

DANA

You're claiming to marry a girl you've never screwed? Don't insult my intelligence.

MR. JACK

I'm telling you the truth. My first priority is no longer sex.

DANA

Well, there's an easy way to test that.

> *Swift as a predator, she embraces him and they meld into the world's most incendiary kiss.*

> *With difficulty,* MR. JACK *pulls away.*

I think you just contradicted yourself.

MR. JACK
(Shakily refilling his glass) Old habits die hard.

DANA
(Baring a breast) Look at me. Tell me you don't want me.

MR. JACK
That's ironic. You never look at me.

> *She knows what he means. She covers herself.*

DANA
(Disingenuously) What do you mean?

MR. JACK
When we make love, you stare past me. Through me.

DANA
I'm looking at you right now.

> *The lure is hard to fight. He almost succumbs.*

MR. JACK
This is not about passion. Look into my eyes. Tell me what you see.

DANA
(She looks away) I don't have to. They're as empty as I feel.

> *The outer door slams.* KATHLEEN *enters.*

You're back early, Kathleen.

KATHLEEN

(Smiles uncertainly) Yes, I just . . . yes, ma'am. I just came back to change clothes. *(She exchanges a meaningful look with* MR. JACK, *then exits.)*

DANA

That dishcloth? Has she looked in your eyes, seen what's there — what's not there?

MR. JACK

(The worst possible answer) Maybe she sees something different.

DANA

I'll fire the bitch.

MR. JACK

Don't take it out on her.

> *The front door slams.*

DANA

(Startled) Leo?!

MR. JACK

What's he doing back so early?

> *With practiced ease, they sit and sort card hands.*

LEO (enters)

Home again, home again, jiggety-jig!

MR. JACK

The play was *that* bad?

LEO

Oh, it was hot stuff. The theatre burned down.

MR. JACK

(Concerned) Are you all right, Leo?

LEO

I'm fine! I heard about it in the cab. I told the driver, turn around, take me home. *(Waves it away)* So how's Dana's bridge game coming?

MR. JACK

Sit in and find out.

LEO

Will do. Give me a moment, let me get comfortable first. *(He exits.)*

DANA

Did you *really* propose to her?

MR. JACK

Yes. This morning.

DANA

I suppose you've told her *all* about us . . .

MR. JACK

Is that a threat?

DANA

Oh, what a *good* idea!

MR. JACK

Dana, please . . . no.

DANA

And how do you plan to stop me?

MR. JACK

I'm begging you, don't.

DANA

Begging? As in, on your knees? Be a little more specific . . .

MR. JACK

I'll do whatever you want.

*He strokes her lips. Her tongue
darts out and licks his fingertip.
It slips between her lips. She
bites. A cry; he snatches back
his hand.*

LEO *reenters wearing a dressing gown.*

LEO

Okay, deal me in.

DANA

Bridge is no fun with only three players.

LEO

So call Kathleen. Maybe she plays.

DANA

(Vehemently) Absolutely not!

LEO

What's your problem?

DANA

She's a servant.

LEO

(Offended) I used to be a servant.

DANA

That's my point.

LEO

What point? Never mind, just deal. I'll take the dummy hand.

LEO *sits between them. She
shuffles.* LEO *cuts. As she deals,*
DANA *speaks oh-so-casually.*

DANA

Leo, brace yourself. Mr. Jack has some *amazing* news.

LEO

What's up?

DANA

He's engaged.

LEO

Ha. Ha. Finish dealing.

DANA

I'm not kidding. He's getting married.

LEO

(Sorts his hand) Yeah, yeah, yeah, yeah, yeah.

MR. JACK

Leo, she's telling you the truth.

LEO

Uh-huh. And I'm the long lost king of Prussia.

DANA

If you say so, your majesty.

LEO

(Studying their faces) You — engaged? Since when?

DANA

This morning.

MR. JACK

(Overlapping) This morning. *(LEO stares, unconvinced.)* Leo, it's true.

LEO

(Suddenly) Oh . . . my . . . *god*! You know what this is? *News*! This is *NEWS!* Brand-new book. Talk shows . . . lecture circuit! Congratulations! *(He hugs him.)*

MR. JACK

Leo, let go of me.

LEO

Who *is* she? Movie star? Princess? Queen? Goddess?

DANA

Stop when you get to the live-in help.

LEO

What?

DANA

You heard.

LEO

Kathleen?

DANA

Kathleen.

LEO

Kathleen?!

MR. JACK

(Nettled) Kathleen.

LEO

Well-ll — *why not?* Real Cinderella story! Yeah! That's good! This calls for a toast!

> *He fetches four glasses and be-*
> *gins filling them with wine.*

DANA

None for me, thanks.

LEO

Don't be a poop. Call Kathleen in here, we'll toast their engagement.

DANA

I am *not* calling Kathleen in here, and I am *not* drinking to their marriage.

LEO

What the hell's your problem?

DANA

You want to know my problem? You want to know my problem?

MR. JACK

(Sensing disaster) Dana . . . !

DANA

Mr. Jack is my lover. That's my problem.

> LEO *very carefully sets down the wine decanter.*

LEO

You want to run that by me again?

DANA

Mr. Jack is my lover. Now he's tired of me and wants to marry the scrublady.

LEO

(Turning to MR. JACK) Why's she doing this? Why's she lying?

DANA

Don't call me a liar! I'm your wife.

LEO

Not if you're telling the truth. *(Quietly)* Mr. J. — I'll believe you.

MR. JACK

Leo . . . I'm sorry.

> LEO *slaps* MR. JACK *and flinches, expecting to get hit.*

>*When nothing happens, he is*
>*convinced.*

I'd better leave.

LEO

You ain't going no-place, mister! Sit down. Both of you!

>*They do as they are told.*

I waited on you hand and foot. You live in my house.

DANA

And who invited him? But look on the bright side, Leo — you can update your book.

LEO

(Glaring) The day we married, every zipper on the West Side flew at half-mast. *(To MR. JACK)* First thing tomorrow, you're history.

MR. JACK

I'll pack right now.

LEO

Not yet you won't. Call in Kathleen. Tell her what you've been doing with my wife.

DANA

Leo!

MR. JACK

I won't do that.

LEO

You won't do that? You won't *do* that? You'll kiss my ass if I tell you to! *(Calls)* KATHLEEN! Tell her the truth, then get out of here, and take this whore from Hell with you! *KATHLEEN!* (DANA *starts to laugh.*) Shut up or I'll break your neck!

DANA

You fell for it! You actually fell for it!

LEO

Fell for what?

DANA

"I *KNOW* jealous husbands!"

MR. JACK

(Catches on) "Most husbands don't act like The Terminator."

LEO

(Mouth agape) No-o!

DANA

(Kneels by MR. J) Please, sir, don't throw out a whore from Hell on a night like this!

MR. JACK

(Histrionically) Go and never darken my door a-gayn! And the curtain falls slowly.

LEO

No!

DANA

Hold on, sports fans, here's the final score: one hit . . .

MR. JACK

Which I took rather well, don't you think?

DANA

No runs . . . and lots of errors.

MR. JACK

Leo, I *do* think you owe playwrights an apology.

> *A doubtful second; then* LEO
> *collapses laughing.*

LEO

You bastards! You world-class bastards!

MR. JACK

My friend, you were positively terrifying.

> DANA *sees* KATHLEEN *enter;*
> *the men do not.*

LEO

God, was I dumb! You and Dana, lovers — ?

DANA

That's so hard to believe? What about Mr. Jack marrying Kathleen?
A man who's slept with movie stars marrying that flat-chested vanilla
milkshake?

> MR. JACK *suddenly realizes*
> KATHLEEN *is there.*

LEO

Dumb, dumber — guilty as charged!

> KATHLEEN *runs off.* MR.
> JACK *looks stunned.*

DANA

(Hands wine glasses to men, keeps one) Weren't you going to propose a toast, Leo?

LEO

To Mr. Jack, patron saint of bachelors. And to my wife, the Queen
of Dirty Tricks!

> *(He and* DANA *drink.* MR.
> JACK *does not.)*

DANA

Now *I* have a toast . . . to my husband and lover.

LEO

I'll drink to that. *(Clinks glasses)* Now how about that game of
bridge?

DANA

Yes, let's. Mr. Jack? *(She tries to steer MR. JACK; he pulls away from her, but sits.)*

LEO

(Studies cards) Dealer passes. Dana?

DANA

One heart. No, make that two.

LEO

(Inspects dummy) Two spades. *(Pause)* Mr. J?

MR. JACK

(Distracted) What?

LEO

Pass. Two hearts. Two spades. Your turn.

MR. JACK

(Staring at DANA) Two — no trump.

SCENE TWO

Later that night. MR. JACK *is sipping scotch.*

LEO

(Entering; in dressing gown) I can't get to sleep.

MR. JACK

I never can.

LEO

Do you always have to be one-up?

MR. JACK

(A small sigh) What's bothering you?

LEO

Your marriage.

MR. JACK

That was a joke.

LEO

But if it wasn't, we could clean up. You could move out, get a place of your own.

MR. JACK

How?

LEO

Another book. Just before getting married, you lay it all out: every one of your secrets, seduction tricks, sex techniques. Think about it — talk shows, DVDs. Who knows? Maybe even Virtual Reality!!

MR. JACK

Apt metaphor for my life. But look, you already wrote everything there is to tell.

LEO

Not your sexual tactics. And not with you telling your own story!

MR. JACK

Leo, I'm not a writer.

LEO

All you have to do is get married. And at the end of the book, you
— ghost-written — explain why none of your other women measure up
to *her.*

MR. JACK

Her? Who? Kathleen?

LEO

Forget Kathleen. Pick a movie star. A princess.

MR. JACK

Royalty requires a pre-nup. Film stars, you have to sleep with their
publicists. *(Sees LEO's expression.)* Figuratively. *(Pause)* Sometimes.
No, if I did agree to this, I'd be better off with a woman nobody knows.
Remember what you said earlier? A Cinderella story. The two of us living under the same roof . . .

> *The door to the sleeping wing*
> *cracks;* KATHLEEN *is listen-*
> *ing.* MR. JACK *sees her;* LEO
> *does not.*

LEO

Come on! Find somebody better looking.

MR. JACK

One afternoon at the salon, Leo, that's all it would take.

LEO

(Suspiciously) You *do* have something going with her!

MR. JACK

She's a woman, she lives here, I noticed. OK, let's do it. Call her in
here, Leo.

> *The door to the wing shuts.*

LEO

At this time of night?

MR. JACK

(Lowers his voice) Catch the enemy off guard . . .

LEO

(Smiles) I haven't heard you say that for a long time!

MR. JACK

Give me a moment to change, then bring her in. *(He exits.)*

LEO

(To audience) OK, earlier, he and Dana were just messing with my head. But I see how she stares at him when she thinks I'm not looking. Him living here is a time bomb. I have got to get him *out!*

> KATHLEEN *enters. She is carrying a suitcase.*

Hey! Where are you going this time of night?

> *She hands him an envelope.*

KATHLEEN

This is my letter of resignation. Please call me a cab.

LEO

Who quits in the middle of the night?

KATHLEEN

Apparently I do. I will not work for people who make fun of me behind my back.

LEO

Uh-oh, what did you hear?

KATHLEEN

The flat-chested vanilla milkshake does not care to discuss it.

LEO

Dana tears everybody apart. But, look, we weren't laughing at you.

KATHLEEN

Sure sounded like it.

LEO

We were laughing at Mr. Jack — the idea of him getting married.

KATHLEEN

Why is that so funny?

> LEO *picks up a book and shows it.*

LEO

Ever read the book I wrote about him?

KATHLEEN

I've been meaning to.

LEO

It's all in here. Girls in every city, town, country. Single, married, divorced; lawyers, nurses, teachers, preachers, nuns who left the church for him. Know how many he's gone to bed with? *(Waits)* Two thousand and sixty-five. It was an answer on *Jeopardy*. And not one pregnancy — yet he never used a condom.

KATHLEEN

He told you *that?*

LEO

Naah. I would've had to buy 'em. *(Mutters)* Slip 'em on and peel 'em off, I bet.

KATHLEEN

Two thousand and sixty-five, but the idea of me and him together made you laugh.

LEO

Not you and him in bed, you and him getting married.

KATHLEEN

(Picks up phone) I'll call my own cab.

LEO

Where you gonna go in the middle of the night?

KATHLEEN

To my sister's. *(Under her breath)* I hate my sister.

LEO

What are you so upset for? *(It dawns)* You really *are* interested in him!

KATHLEEN

Interested in becoming Girl Number two-oh-six-six? No, thanks! *(She dials.)*

LEO

(Takes phone) If you got married you'd be *Wife Number 1.* *(She turns away, upset.)* He *did* propose to you, didn't he? And you said yes. You in love with him?

KATHLEEN

Why do you care?

LEO

I would love to finally get him out of my house.

KATHLEEN

If I went along with your plan, what would I get out of it?

LEO

Pride doesn't carry a price-tag. I learned that working for him.

KATHLEEN

Look, if I marry him, I know you're going to profit from it by writing another book.

LEO

Who told you that?

KATHLEEN

I overheard you talking before.

LEO

Okay, fair enough. Ten percent.

KATHLEEN

Ten percent of what?

LEO

My net earnings.

KATHLEEN

Fifteen percent of gross.

LEO

No way! Twelve, net.

KATHLEEN

For how long?

LEO

What do you mean, how long?

KATHLEEN

How long if it doesn't work and I have to divorce him?

LEO

(Laughs) You are something else. Eighteen months?

KATHLEEN

One year.

LEO

Done deal. He's coming in to talk to you.

KATHLEEN

I know.

LEO

Don't make it too easy, he'll get suspicious.

KATHLEEN

I do not intend to make anything easy for him.

LEO

Shh . . . here he comes.

> MR. JACK *reenters in a silk robe.*

MR. JACK

(To LEO*)* Go upstairs and make sure Dana doesn't interrupt us.

LEO nods and exits.

So how do we begin?

KATHLEEN

Interpret what I heard.

MR. JACK

Dana's viciousness should not be a factor.

KATHLEEN

Never mind. Tell me about princesses. Movie stars. Everyone you've ever slept with.

MR. JACK

That'll take quite a while. What do you want to know?

KATHLEEN

Why I'm not one of them.

MR. JACK

Did you want to be?

KATHLEEN

I'm human. You never tried.

MR. JACK

For the first time in my life, it seemed wrong.

KATHLEEN

Why?

MR. JACK

I don't know.

KATHLEEN

We like Monet and Toscanini and Indian food. Does that add up to marriage?

MR. JACK

I honestly don't know.

KATHLEEN

Normally you're so articulate, but suddenly you've got nothing to say? *(Steps closer to him)* Do you love me?

MR. JACK

I'm not sure what that means. When feelings started kicking in, I always ran the other way. For some reason, this is different. I can't say why.

> *She kisses him. He responds, but without the fervor of his earlier kiss with* DANA.

KATHLEEN

(Steps back) Who is she?

MR. JACK

Everybody. Nobody. Maybe she's got your face.

KATHLEEN

I think I hate you.

MR. JACK

No, you don't.

KATHLEEN

Well, I could hate you for knowing that.

LEO

(Hurries in) Dana's coming down, I couldn't stop her.

MR. JACK

It's all right. She won't interrupt anything.

LEO

What? You blew it?!

MR. JACK

It wasn't a seduction. I have no experience with marriage.

LEO

(Half-pleased, half-upset) The great Mr. Jack blew it?!

MR. JACK

(Pours scotch) I suppose you'll have it on the Six O'Clock News.

> DANA *enters in attractive nightwear.*

DANA

What's everybody doing down here in the middle of the night?

MR. JACK

Sorry if we woke you. We were just having a —

KATHLEEN

(Interrupts) A celebration! *(Takes MR. JACK's arm)* We're getting married.

> LEO *grins.*

> MR. JACK, *surprised and mystified, studies KATHLEEN.*

> DANA *glares at MR. JACK.*

SCENE THREE

A few weeks later. LEO, *looking dapper, is on the phone.* DANA *is pacing.*

LEO

So where are you? How's traffic? Yeah, just honk, we'll be right out. *(Hangs up.)*

DANA

Where is she?

LEO

Just off the 96th Street exit. You could still change your mind and come along.

DANA

Next time, maybe.

LEO

It's his first public lecture. He could use your support.

DANA

Isn't he talking to an all-woman audience?

LEO

Yeah.

DANA

Then he'll be fine. I'm waiting for the new housemaid.

LEO

Oh, right. What's her name? Vivian?

DANA

Violetta.

LEO

How'm I gonna remember that? *(Calls)* Mr. J., hurry up! *(He exits to the wing.)*

DANA

(Clasps hands, looks up) Dear God, I've got a favor to ask. I hardly ever bother you, right? *(Notices audience)* Don't look at me like that. I pray sometimes!

> *Doorbell. She opens it.* VIO-LETTA *enters. She is stunningly attractive, sensuality incarnate — and is the same actor who plays* KATHLEEN.

VIOLETTA

(Hushed) Is Kathy here?

DANA

No. Your room's that way, first door on the left. His is right across from you.

LEO *(reentering)*

Was that the door? *(He sees VIOLETTA and is instantly captivated.)*

DANA

This is Kathleen's replacement.

LEO

(Shakes her hand) Very pleased to meet you . . . uh?

VIOLETTA

Violetta.

LEO

Violetta! *(Still holding her hand)* There's a name I will never forget!

VIOLETTA

And you are — ?

DANA

Off limits. *(They stop holding hands.)* Your outfit's laid out on the bed. Go change.

> VIOLETTA *blows* LEO *a kiss and exits.*

LEO

(After a beat) One day.

DANA

One day what?

LEO

One day before you fire her.

DANA

Probably. So how is Kathleen going to fit into today's lecture?

LEO

The lady who tamed the tiger. She'll make a guest appearance. *(A car horn honks outside.)* There she is. *(Calls)* Mr. J., time to rumble! *(To DANA)* Wish us luck.

DANA

Whatever. *(He exits. Prayer attitude)* All I ask, Lord, is that you end this idiocy. This marriage. Amen. (MR. JACK enters and tries to brush past her, but she blocks his way.) Sooner or later, she's going to find out about us.

MR. JACK

There is no us.

> *She kisses him; he responds like an addict, then pulls away and exits, almost at a run. DANA has a moment of silent agony, then VIOLETTA reenters wearing a sexy outfit.*

VIOLETTA

Kathy wore *this?!*

DANA

Certainly not. I bought it specially for you. Did he see you in it?

VIOLETTA

Oh, yes-s-s. Through my open bedroom door, pulling on my stockings . . . *(She mimes the action)* . . . v-e-r-y s-l-o-w-l-y. Our eyes met . . .

DANA

Good. Now I've got a lecture to get to.

VIOLETTA

Give Kathy Hell!

SCENE FOUR

This theatre. DANA *is seated in the audience.*

LEO

If you haven't handed in your pink cards yet, pass them along now. *(Collects them)* OK, this lecture's for women only. I'm not staying. I just have to make sure no guys snuck in. *(Stares at a man, then shakes head)* Nope, no men in this group. How you like that, girls? Put your hands together, now h-e-eere's Jack! *(Exits)*

MR. JACK *enters, goes to lectern, studies women.*

MR. JACK

A writer claimed there are no "ladies" in America, just women. But nobility reflects spirit, not pedigree, so I'll begin by saying, ladies, thank you for coming. Now let's share some secrets. *(He selects a pink card.)* Jeanette asks, "How can you find something appealing in every woman?" *(Smiles at them singly and collectively)* Look at you . . . how can I *not* be charmed? Women raised me. When I was weak, they were strong. All my life, I've tried to show my gratitude. I thank whatever gods may be there's a feminine side to me as well.

(Another card) Evelyn asks, "Do you find pregnant women attractive?" Whenever I see a pregnant woman, I want to hug her. She carries the precious gift of new life, an activity rich in tenderness and love.

DON JUAN *now answers 2-3 of the cards audience members filled out. (Briskly paced, please!) Naturally the actor must be skilled at ad libbing in character, in the manner of a magician, hypnotist or improvisational comedian.*

(Another card) Now this card is from Dominique. What a lovely name . . . where are you, Dominique? *(He drafts a MAN from the audience.)* Please come forward. *(Hands "her" the card.)* Dominique, your

question deserves special attention . . . please read it aloud? Big voice, please, so everyone can hear . . .

"DOMINIQUE"

"Of all the women you've known before your fianceé, who meant the most to you?"

MR. JACK

Her name was Angelica. And it's uncanny, but — no, I'll tell you in a moment. Leo?

> *He snaps his fingers. LEO enters with a stool, which he places near the lectern, then exits.*
>
> MR. JACK *guides* "DOMINIQUE", *seating* "her" *on the stool and standing beside* "her". "She" *is seated with back to the audience.*
>
> *In this sequence,* MR. JACK *reveals his skill as a seducer. He lowers voice, takes* "her" *hand and talks to* "DOMINIQUE" *as if the audience did not exist. He never takes his eyes off* "her", *and uses the hypnotist trick of seeming to look into* "her" *but really staring at a point in mid-forehead and an inch within, as if he had X-ray vision.*

Dominique, do you live in town, or are you visiting?

> *"She" replies. He asks ad lib questions to evoke personal facts. At the first likely opportunity, he interrupts an answer.*

Please allow me . . . a little speck of makeup . . . *(His fingertips brush "her" cheek as if removing a speck.)* You asked which woman was my favorite — the strange thing is, you remind me of her. Angelica. The identical complexion. The same eyes, the same look — but the thing that reminds me of her the most is your smile. More dazzling than the sun . . . but you've heard that before, right? *(If No, he replies, "*Never? Then it's time you did!*" If Yes, he says, "*Of course you have!*")* If she were here now . . . *(On his knees)* . . . and it's almost as if she were . . . *(Cups "her" face, captivated, but stops.)* But I'm engaged now, it would be wrong to kiss you. You'd best be seated.

> *"She" returns to her seat.* MR. JACK*'s tone abruptly changes.*

Confession time. There never was an Angelica. Or maybe there was, Leo would know, he's got my list. Before Kathleen, *every* woman was my favorite because every woman is unique. Sadly, few of you believe that. Sorry if I embarrassed you, Dominique, but I want you to know I see your inner — and outer — loveliness.

> *Blows "her" a kiss, then holds up another card.*

One more question . . . Elizabeth wants to know what's the biggest sexual turn-on for me. Feeling a woman's pleasure, knowing I'm the author. What they say at Christmas is true — it *is* better to give than to receive.

DANA

That is such bullshit!

MR. JACK

(Startled, sees her for the first time) I didn't think you were coming.

DANA

Women are a power trip to you. That's what turns *you* on!

> LEO *pokes his head out, surprised she is there.*

MR. JACK

(A warning hint) And how would *you* know that?

DANA *(sees LEO)*

I read Leo's book. *(LEO goes.)* Forget what turns you on. What's in it for women?

MR. JACK

Technique. Statistics don't lie.

DANA

Oh, yes, your precious list of women's names. Where would you be without it?

MR. JACK

I am the direct descendant of Don Juan. I inherited my character from him.

DANA

Now how's that possible? The way I heard the story, he died childless.

MR. JACK *(counting off on his fingers)*

My great-great-great-great-grandfather was born out of wedlock.

DANA

So you come from a long line of figurative *and* literal bastards. No wonder you get such bad PR.

MR. JACK

Writers glamorize us, as long as they send us to Hell in the last act. I'm proud of my kin: Don Juan, Don Joo-Ann, Don Giovanni, John Tanner. Each one dedicated to mankind's greatest riddle: *Das Ewig-Weibliche.* The eternal feminine.

DANA

Only a man could come up with such a dumb idea. So have you solved the riddle?

MR. JACK

It's unsolvable. Men want to learn my "knack," but it's not a skill, it's an art.

DANA

The art of meaningless sex.

MR. JACK

(Turns away) I'd like to introduce my fiancée. *(Calls)* Kathleen? *(She enters; he indicates a handful of cards)* Several women want to know how we met.

KATHLEEN

I was curious about you. One day you were in the parlour reading Proust —

MR. JACK

Trying to read Proust.

KATHLEEN

— and I came in to dust. I said, "Am I disturbing you?"

MR. JACK

Quite pleasantly.

KATHLEEN

I was warned about you.

MR. JACK

So I'm dangerous? *(She nods.)* Does that make you worry?

KATHLEEN

No. I just feel sorry for you.

MR. JACK

(After a beat) I'd like to know why.

KATHLEEN

You already know. Just because I'm a woman — that's enough?

MR. JACK

It's never enough.

KATHLEEN

But you'd like it to be.

MR. JACK

How do you know things about me I hardly admit to myself?

KATHLEEN

Is that supposed to flatter me?

MR. JACK

Does it?

KATHLEEN

You know it does.

MR. JACK

(To audience) Which is when I realized she both fascinated and frightened me.

DANA

(Interrupting) Kathy, is it true you've got a baby sister?

KATHLEEN

(After a dead silence) I have a sister. She's younger.

DANA

Is she as pretty?

MR. JACK

What are you doing?!

KATHLEEN

I'll answer her. My mother used to tell me, incessantly — "Violetta inherited *my* good looks. *You* got your daddy's brains." That used to bother me. It doesn't any more.

MR. JACK

End of digression. A few nights after the first time we met, Kathleen came home and I saw she'd been crying. "What did he do to you?"

KATHLEEN

It's that obvious?

MR. JACK

I'm supposed to be an expert.

KATHLEEN

All right. We had this long talk. *(Sighs)* Why did it have to get so complicated?

MR. JACK

Translation: you used the "L" word. It scared him off.

KATHLEEN

That's what I get for being a romantic.

MR. JACK

No, that's what you get for being a first stage romantic.

KATHLEEN

And according to you, how many stages *are* there?

MR. JACK

Three. First stage: you believe in love, in tender emotions, happy endings, all the Hallmark valentines. Then you learn — bliss leads to pain, disappointment, mind-games, power trips, arguments, lies. You stop believing in love. That's the second stage . . . *(looks at audience)* . . . where most of you folk hang out.

KATHLEEN

But you claim there's a third stage?

MR. JACK

Yes. But before you get there, you wrap daily routine round your shoulders like a horsehair blanket. Which is both comforting and irritating. Life becomes predictable. No joy, no epiphanies, day after day after day . . . until you finally tell yourself, maybe love doesn't really work, but isn't it better than a world where nothing sings or sparkles? So you risk opening your heart again, and when the contradictions come — and they *always* come — you look the other way and pretend love is still working . . . and that's how you become a third stage romantic.

KATHLEEN

Even when it hurts?

MR. JACK

Especially when it hurts.

> *They almost kiss.* MR. JACK
> *turns to audience.*

At which point, I abruptly said good night, and went to my room.

KATHLEEN

My second rejection that day, and this time from a man who'd slept with thousands. I went to bed and cried a lot.

MR. JACK

I was right across the hall. I heard.

KATHLEEN

You were meant to.

DANA

So when did you start sleeping with each other?

KATHLEEN

That is none of your fu — *(Pause; she self-edits)* — business!

DANA

After you're married, he'll cheat on you.

MR. JACK

I won't!

KATHLEEN

(Overlapping) He will not!

DANA

Read my husband's book. Quote. It's never the one you have, it's always the one you don't have *yet.* Unquote.

KATHLEEN

I trust him.

DANA

Because he loves you?

KATHLEEN

He's never told me that. *(Turns to him.)* That's your cue.

MR. JACK

(Too long a pause) What *is* love? Eskimos have so many words for snow, but we've only got this one for the heart's most complicated emotion.

DANA

That's what you're going to marry. But if you love him, I guess that'll be enough.

KATHLEEN

Actually I don't.

MR. JACK

Don't . . . what?

KATHLEEN

I don't love you. *(Kisses his cheek)* I'm just a third stage romantic.

He stares at her, then laughs.

Blackout.

SCENE FIVE

The living room, later.

KATHLEEN *and* DANA *enter.*
LEO, *in mid-tirade, is right behind them.*

LEO

What got into you? There were reporters! How could you say that
to him?

KATHLEEN

Headlines, talk shows. Next week I change my mind, "I *do* love
him." More air time.

*He laughs, enlightened, but then
turns to* DANA.

LEO

You, though, you say you're not coming, all of a sudden you pop up,
tear into him.

A car horn blares outside.

DANA

Leo, pay the taxi.

LEO

This is not finished!

DANA

And while you're out, go to Zabar's, pick up something for break-
fast.

The car horn sounds again.

LEO

You are incredible! *(Exits)*

DANA

Whatever. *(She faces* KATHLEEN.*)* Well.

KATHLEEN

Well. Stop being my enemy.

DANA

You flatter yourself.

KATHLEEN

What were you trying to do?

DANA

Give you some good sisterly advice.

KATHLEEN

I don't need another sister.

DANA

Friendly advice, then.

KATHLEEN

OK, here's some for you — let him go.

DANA

Excuse me?!

KATHLEEN

Keep acting like a loose cannon, and even your husband is going to catch on.

DANA

(After a beat) I'm going to have a brandy. Want one?

KATHLEEN

The lady of the house pours the servant girl a drink? How can I refuse?

DANA

You have moved up a bit. *(Pours)* In England, they call it "jumped up." It's not a compliment. *(Hands her the drink)* So what should we drink to?

KATHLEEN

Honesty?

DANA

All right, here's some. He *will* cheat on you.

KATHLEEN

No, he won —

DANA

(Overtalks) I don't mean someday he'll fall into his old habits. I'm saying he'll cheat on you first chance he gets. Possibly this evening.

KATHLEEN

You're going to try to sleep with him tonight?

DANA

Kathleen, for shame! I'm happily married. But have you met our new housemaid?

> KATHLEEN *stares at her sus-*
> *piciously, then exits to the wing.*
> *She returns, stunned.*

Violetta. So exotic. Kathleen. So lace curtain. Ah, well . . . what's in a name?

KATHLEEN

You're despicable.

DANA

You forgot to lisp. *(Like Daffy Duck)* "You're dethhhpicable!"

KATHLEEN

Stop it!

DANA

What's the big whoop if he nails your sister? You told him you don't love him.

MR. JACK

(Enters; sternly) Dana, go to bed.

DANA

Oh, do the little love birds want privacy? Absolutement! *(Switches on the FM; soft romantic music.)* Now behave yourselves, you're not married yet. *(Blows kiss, exits)*

KATHLEEN

(A longish pause) Have you met my sister?

MR. JACK

What?

KATHLEEN

My sister. Across the hall from you.

MR. JACK

Oh, my God! The new maid?

KATHLEEN

Violetta.

MR. JACK

That's why Dana asked you about her.

KATHLEEN

She says I can't trust you.

MR. JACK

So what? You don't love me.

KATHLEEN

You couldn't tell if I did.

MR. JACK

It hurt when you said it.

KATHLEEN

It hurt? You laughed.

MR. JACK

Laughter. Tears. The same exact muscles.

KATHLEEN

(To audience) That he knows about! *(Starts for the door)* Good night.

MR. JACK

Don't go.

KATHLEEN

Give me one good reason.

MR. JACK

Could I love you? Yes. Could I love someone else? Yes. And you're exactly the same. Our choices — altogether arbitrary.

KATHLEEN

(After a beat) Don Juan, this may be a first — but you just struck out.

MR. JACK

Kathleen . . . I *need* you!

KATHLEEN

(She is touched, but her tone is gently ironic) The cry of a soul in torment?

MR. JACK

Yes. Possibly — genuine.

KATHLEEN

Possibly — arbitrary.

MR. JACK

We both know that.

KATHLEEN

(Hushed) I'll stay. *(With as much reluctance as desire, she embraces him. They stare into each other's eyes. After a long moment . . .)* You touch me with such reverence.

MR. JACK

Trust that. Not my words.

> *Their bodies meld; they kiss. Music up. Blackout. After about ten seconds, the music diminishes, the lights come up; MR. JACK is with VIOLETTA.*

VIOLETTA

Where's Kathy?

MR. JACK

(Lying) She . . . went home.

> *He kisses her; their bodies meld.*

VIOLETTA

You touch me with such reverence.

> *Music up.*
>
> *Blackout.*

ACT TWO

SCENE ONE

> *Immediately afterward.* MR.
> JACK *and* VIOLETTA *are still*
> *kissing.*

MR. JACK

(Drawing away from her) This is wrong.

VIOLETTA

Come back here.

> *She pulls him back; they kiss*
> *even more passionately, but with*
> *great effort he stops.*

MR. JACK

I can't.

VIOLETTA

Don't make me the one woman you pushed away.

MR. JACK

Violetta, I'm sorry. You're very beautiful, but I just figured something out. Finally.

VIOLETTA

What?

MR. JACK

Intimacy has to be earned.

> *He exits to his bedroom.* DANA
> *enters immediately.*

DANA

He's trying to grow a conscience. It won't take. Go after him!

VIOLETTA

I don't chase after men, not even him.

DANA

Not even to spite Kathy?

VIOLETTA

Not even. I've got my pride.

DANA

I didn't hire you for your pride.

VIOLETTA

You didn't hire me. I volunteered.

DANA

I said I'd pay you.

> LEO *appears, coming from out-*
> *side.*

VIOLETTA

If I took your money, what would that make me?

LEO

I thought it made you the maid.

DANA

Violetta apparently has her own agenda. She hired on to seduce him.

LEO

Seduce who?

DANA

(Dryly) Not you, darling.

LEO

Jack in the sack? Now he's got groupies?

DANA

Leo . . . see it as an opportunity.

LEO

I'm listening.

DANA

The same night Kathleen says she doesn't love him, Mr. Jack sleeps with her sister.

LEO

You're her *sister?* That's what I call sibling rivalry!

VIOLETTA

"Never mind, Vee-Vee. You got Mama's good looks, your sister got Daddy's brains." You know how many times I had to hear that?

LEO

So you came here to stab her in the back.

VIOLETTA

Plus I read your book. Made me wonder if any man's that good.

DANA

Well, you won't find out. Kathleen's got him all sewed up.

VIOLETTA

Wouldn't be the first time I took a man away from her.

DANA

You're talking about a one-night stand, right?

VIOLETTA

If he's that good, maybe a little longer.

LEO

Two weeks, that's his average.

DANA

Just how much do you want to piss off Kathleen?

VIOLETTA

That number has not been invented.

DANA

So why don't you marry him?

VIOLETTA

Reality check — he's engaged to her.

DANA

Not if she catches the two of you in bed.

VIOLETTA

I know, but . . . I tried. He pushed me away.

DANA

"Old habits die hard." I quote. Try again. Right now. Catch the enemy off guard.

LEO *looks at her oddly.*

VIOLETTA

OK, I guess it's worth one more try . . . *(She exits.)*

DANA

Leo, how can you be so cruel — doing this to poor little Kathleen?

LEO

Fuck her. No marriage, no twelve per cent.

VIOLETTA

(Returning) I heard that. If this works out, I'll accept ten.

LEO

Deal. Now get back to Jack.

VIOLETTA

I can't. His door's locked.

LEO

I'll get you the key. *(Exits upstairs.)*

DANA

Not a word to Leo.

VIOLETTA

Your vendetta is perfectly safe. But what about me?

DANA

What do you mean?

VIOLETTA

If I *do* get him into bed, are you going to rip my eyes out afterwards?

DANA

I'll get through it somehow.

VIOLETTA

Ain't love grand . . .

DANA

Love, my ass — he's an addiction.

VIOLETTA

(To herself) Why is that not a comfort?

> LEO *reenters with several keys on a key-ring.*

LEO

This one. *(VIOLETTA takes it and exits.)* Do you think she'll —

DANA

Shh! I'm listening.

> *A pause.* VIOLETTA *returns, looking grim.*

VIOLETTA

Lying bastard told me Kathy went home.

LEO

Oh, shit! They're together?

> *She nods. All three think for a moment.*

DANA

(Snaps her fingers) Your parents, are they in good health?

VIOLETTA

Daddy's got a heart condition . . . Oh! That *is* vicious! Can I change in your room?

DANA

Go!

> VIOLETTA *nods, runs to her room, runs back with sexy nightwear and then exits upstairs.*

Leo, you have to do it. Kathleen doesn't trust me.

LEO

Do what?

DANA

Oh god, you are *so* dense! Tell her the bad news!

> *Suddenly enlightened, he nods and runs out. We hear a knock, and then his voice, offstage.*

LEO

Mr. J.? Is Kathy in there with you?

> DANA *pours a shot of brandy.* LEO *reenters, followed by* KATHLEEN *hastily dressing.*

KATHLEEN

How bad is it? Is Daddy still — ?

DANA

Your sister didn't say.

KATHLEEN

Where is Vee-Vee?

DANA

LaGuardia. She went ahead to buy tickets. *(Offers drink)* Here. Steady your nerves.

KATHLEEN

(Drinking) Thanks.

DANA

Leo will drive you.

LEO

I will?

KATHLEEN

You're being so nice, both of you! Thanks — let me get my purse. *(Runs out)*

LEO

Why'd you have to volunteer me? Middle of the night, she couldn't grab a cab?

DANA

Because you've got to tell us when you're on the way back. How long can you stall?

LEO

This late, no traffic, we'll be there in fifteen. Then what?

DANA

Play dumb. She'll think her sister lied.

LEO

And then?

DANA

And then call us and bring her back as fast as you can.

LEO

You are incredible! *(He hugs her. She endures it.)*

KATHLEEN *returns with* MR.
JACK, *who looks tense.*

KATHLEEN

I'm ready. *(KATHLEEN hugs MR. JACK, then exits with LEO.)*

DANA

Have a safe trip. *(She recognizes MR. JACK's condition.)* Bad timing, was it?

MR. JACK

I could use a scotch. A double.

DANA

(She pours one, brings it, dips a finger, runs it over his lips.) Sleep well, chere amie . . .

She exits. He watches her go, drains his glass.

A scantily-clad VIOLETTA *comes downstairs. Arrested by the sight, he can neither move nor resist as she takes possession of him.*

BLACKOUT

SCENE TWO

This theatre several months later. LEO enters.

LEO

Tonight is a first. I worked for months and Mr. Jack finally agreed to talk to just men this one and only time! Tomorrow he gets married, so you're his bachelor party. Now trust me — if anybody here took Viagra tonight, y'better leave before Mr. J. introduces his new bride to be. Now he-e-e-ere's Jack! *(Goes to side, watches.)*

A tired MR. JACK enters with blue cards.

MR. JACK

(Dourly) I've read your questions. Most of them are blatantly sexual. For instance, this — person — asks whether I prefer "T" or "A." Whose card is this? *(Pretends to see a hand.)* Stand up. Do you know the chemical constituency of a woman's body? *I* don't. If we *did* know, would it improve our love lives? Of course not. You can't reduce anything as complex as a woman to the sum of her parts. Now sit down.

(Holds up card) "Mostly I like skinny girls, but pregnant women turn me on. How come?" Assuming the mother-to-be you're eager for is not your own wife, there are three reasons. She's sexually experienced, you can't impregnate her, and if you succeed in cheating with her, what really arouses you is the skill of your iniquity.

Here MR. JACK may answer a "blatantly sexual" audience card. (But he must keep it brief!)

(Holds up card) This one, at least, is a bit more sophisticated. "What is the inherent pleasure of 'frottage.'" *(He studies faces.)* Leo, definition . . .

MR. JACK pronounces it correctly, frah-

TAZH. LEO *mispronounces it:*
FRAH-tij.

LEO

Frottage: rubbing up against strangers. Y'know — IRT at rush hour.

MR. JACK

What is its inherent pleasure? Guilt. A coward's version of rape. I'm only guessing.

LEO

Come on, don't tell me you never did it!

MR. JACK

Sorry, its appeal never . . . rubbed off on me. And I don't like these questions, either.

LEO

You promised.

MR. JACK

Fine. Take notes. Gentlemen, you're all afraid of the critical moment when directly or indirectly, you ask a woman to accept you into herself. It's upsetting enough always having to be the ones who ask, but rejection, no matter how gently she may say No, is what Marie Antoinette called one of life's little deaths. Some men hear one No too many and become rapists; some offer themselves up as slaves, hoping for table-scraps of passion. Some turn to other men, I suppose. But all my life I have devoted myself to the crusade of changing the next painful No to a resounding Yes.

LEO

That's what we're all here to learn how to do.

MR. JACK

You think so? *(Reads)* "What's the best pickup line?" That's what *they* came for.

LEO

Well, what's the answer?

MR. JACK

Pickup lines suck. Play reporter: get her to talk about herself. Remember to listen!

LEO

What if she's boring?

MR. JACK

Will her pussy be as boring as her prattle?

LEO

Pussy?! You never talk like that!

MR. JACK

I'm playing to my audience. *(Wearily)* I'm telling you what to do, but you won't believe me. You have to learn to appeal to a woman's mind.

LEO

Ahh, come on!

MR. JACK

You want expert advice? Here it is — Reinvent your egos. Give up your adolescent obsession with sports; learn the infinitely more challenging game of seduction. *Study the enemy!* Become blank canvas and paint yourself how women want to see you. Become the apology for all other men. *That* is my entire secret.

LEO

Aaw, look, I worked for you for a long time. You used all kinds of tricks.

MR. JACK

I have tactics, yes, but they won't work if you don't accept what I just told you.

LEO

Let me be the judge! *(Waves hand at audience)* Us! These guys!

MR. JACK

Tactics, you want tactics — all right. Pretend you're a woman, Leo.

LEO
What?

MR. JACK
You heard. Make believe you're a woman. *(Pause)* I mean it!

> LEO *walks with an exaggerated wiggle.*

MR. JACK *(Cont.)*
You're doing a parody. Pretend you're at one of my "women only" lectures. I've just called you onstage. What thoughts are racing through your mind?

LEO
Ooh, they're all looking at me! My dress is wrinkled! I'm having a bad hair day!

MR. JACK

You're being a clown. Still, we'll assume you're right. I see your discomfort and channel it. I focus all my attention on you . . . I take your hand . . .

> *He does so.* LEO *giggles.*

If you can't take this seriously, I won't do it.

LEO
It's embarrassing!

MR. JACK
All right. I'll get somebody else. *(Looks at audience)* I need a man who won't feel threatened pretending to be a woman for a few moments. *(Points)* You, sir — please.

> *He brings a* WOMAN *onstage. He seats "him" as "DOMI-NIQUE" was seated in Act I.*

Let's pretend your name is Dominique. Now when you come up here, I have you sit down facing away from the audience. Leo, have you figured out why?

LEO

So she can only focus on you.

MR. JACK

Correct. *(To "him")* Now I talk to you, ask questions, draw you out. I stroke your cheek. That, plus the fact you're sitting and I'm standing raises my status and lowers yours. *(Strokes cheek)* Doesn't that feel good? *(Instructs "him")* Say yes. *(To audience)* They always do. *(Prompting "him")* "Yes, it feels nice!"

"DOMINIQUE"

Yes, it feels nice.

MR. JACK

Excellent. You even sound like a woman. He's better than you, Leo. Now, pay attention. When you touch a woman, imagine you're in church. An act of reverence. Sometimes I brush my fingers lightly against her earlobes: they're very sensitive. When I look into her eyes, I employ a stare I learned from a hypnotist.

> DANA *enters, hands* LEO *a book, exits.*

LEO

To learn how to stare like Mr. Jack, buy a copy of *Mr. Jack -- For Better or For Worse,* on sale in the lobby of this theatre.

MR. JACK

(To "Dominique") Thank you, sir. Now if you were a woman, I'd get you to hug me before sending you back to your seat, but *I'm* not going there, so please sit down.

> "DOMINIQUE" *sits down.*
> LEO *holds up a blue card.*

LEO

Mr. J., here's a question I'd *really* like to hear you answer. It's not in your book.

MR. JACK

Read it to me.

LEO

(Reads) "How did you screw so many girls, but never knock anyone up?"

MR. JACK

I'm sorry, but that's one secret I'm never going to reveal.

LEO

(To the audience) Hey, I tried. *(With a shrug, he exits.)*

MR. JACK

A few of you asked about my former fianceé, Kathleen. I'm not comfortable talking about her, though I do understand your curiosity.

VIOLETTA *enters.*

VIOLETTA

I'll tell them about her. Kathy couldn't hold on to you. *(He glares.)* Introduce me . . .

MR. JACK

This is Kathleen's sister.

VIOLETTA

(Forcing a smile) I'm Violetta, Mr. Jack's fianceé. *(A beat)* His current fianceé.

MR. JACK

(Dryly) Who loves me very much.

VIOLETTA

Of course I do!

MR. JACK

As much as you love your little business arrangement with Leo?

LEO

(Offstage) HEY!!

VIOLETTA

Leo didn't ask me to marry you. You did!

MR. JACK

That's absolutely true. And it is, was, and always will be a monstrous mistake.

> MR. JACK *exits.* VIOLETTA *is stunned.* LEO *hurries back onstage.*

LEO

Cold feet! Night-before cold feet! Go after him! *(No response)* GO *AFTER HIM!*

> She exits. LEO *gapes at the audience, tongue-tied.* DANA *enters, whispers. He nods, exits.*

DANA

Leo's right. Prenuptial jitters. Meanwhile, look, Mr. Jack lived in my house for years, I can answer a few questions . . . *(She picks a card)* "Do you prefer blondes, brunettes, or redheads?" Definitely — *(Names her own color and picks another card.)* "Who's the worst lover you've ever had?" We could get into legal trouble naming names — *(She looks anxiously offstage.)* Leo? What's happening? *(Louder)* LEO!

> No reply. She reads another card as LEO *appears.*

One more question. "Mr. J., after you make love, what do you like to talk about?" Nothing. He never says a goddamn word. *(She realizes what she just said.)* Oh, shit!

> She sees LEO. *They stare at one another.*

BLACKOUT

SCENE THREE

The living room, later that night. The phone is ringing. MR. JACK *enters from outside, removes coat, answers.*

MR. JACK

Yes? Mr. Jack isn't at home. No, neither is he. Neither is she. *(Hangs up. It rings again.)* What? No comment . . . what part of no comment don't you understand?

He slams it down, disconnects it. He pours himself a scotch, goes to card table, deals, loses interest. The outside door opens; VIOLETTA *storms in.*

VIOLETTA

Why'd you do that to me!?

MR. JACK

If I had a dollar for every time I've been asked that.

VIOLETTA

We had a deal.

MR. JACK

Your deal was with Leo.

VIOLETTA

I'll sue you!

MR. JACK

You won't get much. The new book's not selling. My 15 minutes are up. I'm passé.

VIOLETTA

Also impotent.

MR. JACK
Don't take it personally.

VIOLETTA
Believe me, I don't! World's greatest lover! Hah! When's the last time you got it up?

MR. JACK
(Pause) With your sister.

> *She snatches his drink, almost throws it, but stops to sip it. Wetting her fingers, she flicks a few drops at him, takes a larger sip and hands glass back to him.*

That was uncommonly civilized of you.

VIOLETTA
Well, it *is* the thirty-year-old. Why did you walk offstage?

MR. JACK
I suddenly choked on the lies.

VIOLETTA
I read Leo's book. There's nothing in it about you having a conscience.

MR. JACK
It's comparatively recent.

VIOLETTA
Are you actually in love with her?

MR. JACK
How can I answer that? I do *not* know what love is.

VIOLETTA
Sometimes you pretend you do.

MR. JACK
Pretending? Well, that's something you certainly know about.

VIOLETTA

Excuse me?

MR. JACK

Your sensuality . . . totally studied. A technique you use to control men, but keep them at a distance.

VIOLETTA

Why would I do that?

MR. JACK

Because real intimacy terrifies you. Which, believe me, I understand all too well.

DANA

(Rushes in, agitated) Mr. J., we've got to talk!

VIOLETTA

That's my cue to get lost. *(She starts toward the front door.)*

MR. JACK

Where are you going this time of night?

VIOLETTA

As if you care.

MR. JACK

I wouldn't have asked if I didn't.

VIOLETTA

(Winces) Know what you are? A poison dart disguised as a Tinker-toy. I got stuck. But I'll survive. I hardly felt the prick. *(She exits.)*

MR. JACK

(Sees DANA's impatience) What?!

DANA

After you left, I filled in answering your cards. I slipped and said something bad.

MR. JACK

About us? *(She nods.)* And Leo heard? *(She nods)* At long last, an end to the lying.

DANA

That's hardly a benefit!

MR. JACK

Why does it matter to you? Your marriage is a joke.

DANA

Quoth the expert?

MR. JACK

You treat Leo with utter contempt.

DANA

Which is what he expects. Which you conditioned him for.

MR. JACK

Don't blame me for your connubial bliss.

DANA

Up yours! Are you going to help me?

MR. JACK

Hard to resist, put like that. Why should I? It's your fault I lost Kathleen.

DANA

Which you should thank me for. *(He glares.)* OK, help me out, we'll get her back.

MR. JACK

A little late for that.

DANA

Nothing's too late till you're dead. I am begging you — don't let me lose Leo!

MR. JACK

Leo, or his bank account?

DANA

Be cynical on your own time!

The outside door slams.

Oh, God, he's home!

MR. JACK

Go upstairs! Now! *(She exits. As he refills his glass, he addresses the audience.)* She screws up, I'm supposed to fix it. Saving a marriage! This is a first!

LEO

(Stalks on ready to kill) Don't you ever drink the blended?!

MR. JACK

Glen Turret, it's my favorite. You order it for me specially.

LEO

Just one of the little perks, living in my house.

MR. JACK

You've always been generous.

LEO

Now there's an understatement. *(Suddenly notices)* Why's the phone unplugged?

MR. JACK

The press has become a nuisance. You're angry at me for walking offstage, right?

LEO

That's old news. Didn't Dana tell you?

MR. JACK

Tell me what? She came in upset, but I was talking to Violetta, Dana went upstairs.

LEO

Where's Violetta?

MR. JACK

Gone.

LEO

After you walked, Dana started answering some of your questions. One asked what you like to talk about after sex. She knew the answer.

MR. JACK

Oh, Leo, come on, she lied before about being my lover, remember?

LEO

She wasn't lying this time.

MR. JACK

Book sales are down, lectures ditto. Wouldn't you expect something outrageous from her to turn things around?

LEO

I saw her face when she said it. She wasn't faking.

MR. JACK

Dana is a good actress.

LEO

(Louder) Stop bullshitting! I saw her face!

MR. JACK *(after a long pause)*

All right. It's true.

LEO

You bastard! You went broke, I invited you into my house. I fed you, I bought you new clothes, I stocked your favorite scotch. For thanks, you screw my wife!

MR. JACK

Now who's bullshitting? You invited me out of spite. The lower I fell, the higher you soared. Theatre critic! Didn't catch a trick straight out of Restoration comedy.

LEO

I love Dana! That meant zilch to you!

MR. JACK

Love her? You can't even say her name right, "Day-nah!" It's Dana.

LEO

That's the way *you* pronounce it!

MR. JACK

Leo, how many times did she try to correct you before she gave it up? I heard her.

LEO *(after an angry pause)*

I'm going upstairs. If you're smart, you won't be here when I get back. *(Exits)*

> MR. JACK *finishes his drink, begins to leave, but* KATHLEEN *is standing in the doorway. Her hair now resembles her sister's. A moment of wonder.*

Kathleen! What are you doing here?

KATHLEEN *(enters, closing door)*

My sister called and asked if she could stay overnight. She told me what happened.

MR. JACK

You changed your hair.

KATHLEEN

Do you like it?

MR. JACK

Better the old way.

KATHLEEN

That was the right answer. *(Smiles)* Which of course you knew.

DANA *runs in.*

DANA

What did you say to Leo? He's looking for my pistol! What's she doing here?

KATHLEEN

You have a pistol?!

MR. JACK

She's from Dallas. *(To DANA)* Is he going to find it?

LEO

(Enters with small pistol) Oh, yeah! Hey . . . Kathleen! Looking good!

DANA

That's mine. Give it back.

LEO

No way, baby.

MR. JACK

Leo, sorry for the cliché, but it would hurt you more than it would me.

LEO

Not where I'm aiming . . .

> KATHLEEN *steps in front of* MR. JACK.

MR. JACK

Kathleen, get out of the way!

KATHLEEN

No. If you shoot him, you shoot me!

> *But* MR. JACK *gently pushes her aside.*

MR. JACK

Leo, earlier tonight you asked me a question I said I wouldn't answer.

LEO

What are you talking about?

MR. JACK

You asked how I could sleep with so many women, but never get anyone pregnant.

LEO

What's that got to do with you screwing my wife?

MR. JACK

This is my last secret, Leo. When Dana and I made love . . . *(He stops.)*

LEO

Yeah? When you made love — *what?*

MR. JACK

I never came. *(Brief pause)* I almost never do.

> DANA *stiffens.* LEO's *jaw drops.*

LEO

You expect me to believe that*?!*

MR. JACK

Would I admit it if it wasn't true? Would any man? Even to avoid a bullet?

LEO

You shagged thousands!

MR. JACK

It happened now and then, but not often. And never with your wife.

LEO

But look at Day-nah! *(Corrects himself)* Dah-nah! How could you *not* come?

DANA

Obviously he's lying!

MR. JACK

Women don't hold a monopoly on faking orgasms.

LEO

More bullshit! Wouldn't she have noticed something — missing?

MR. JACK

Leo, Leo, women are so easily fooled.

LEO

I'd like to know how.

MR. JACK

All you need is some saliva on your fingertips.

DANA

(Seizing the gun) If you won't shoot him, *I* will!

LEO

Hey! Don't!

DANA

Back off, Leo! And don't *you* stand in front of him again, or I'll shoot you both.

LEO

You're crazy! I wasn't really going to pull the trigger! I just wanted to scare him!

DANA

Scare him? *(She fires. MR. JACK is unhurt.)* I wanted him to wet his pants.

LEO

Well, you missed. *I* did. *(He runs upstairs.)*

MR. JACK

Did you miss deliberately?

DANA

It only fires blanks. Hmm — what does that remind me of? *(She exits.)*

> MR. JACK *pours scotch, downs it neat. He offers one to* KATH-LEEN; *she declines.*

MR. JACK

That was very foolish, standing in front of me. And you don't even love me.

KATHLEEN

You couldn't tell if I did.

MR. JACK

I'll tell you this, though. All the months not seeing you: the books we talked about, I couldn't bear to look at. Music we listened to grew dissonant. Riverside Park — no matter how bright the sun, no matter how many people were out on a Sunday, to me it was always cold, grey, empty. That I swear is true. I just can't tell you I love you.

KATHLEEN

What do you think you just did?

> MR. JACK *winces. She wisely channels his emotion into a kiss. He steps back, no further, though, than arm's-length.*

MR. JACK

But I slept with your sister . . .

KATHLEEN

Will that ever happen again?

MR. JACK

(Painful honesty) Not with your sister. Hopefully only you. I'm trying to be honest —

KATHLEEN

I know what you're saying. I understand who you are.

MR. JACK

And you — still . . . ?

KATHLEEN

I'll try to. That's all I can promise.

MR. JACK

I . . . *(A long pause)* . . . love you.

KATHLEEN

(Smiling) Duh.

> *They kiss like first-stage roman-tics.*

> LEO, *his pants changed, enters.*

LEO

I would appreciate you getting the hell out of here.

MR. JACK

Just so you know: Kathleen and I *are* getting married. *(Quickly)* We are, aren't we?

KATHLEEN *(laughs)*

You better believe it! *(To LEO)* By the way — you owe me twelve percent, net!

> *They exit.* LEO *looks round the room.*

LEO

Oh, Willy, Willy, I made the last payment on the house today. We're *free*! *(A joyful whoop.)*

> DANA *enters. She is in attractive night-wear.*

DANA

Something worth shouting about?

LEO

He's finally outta here! For the first time, our home is actually *our* home. Gotta admit, though, his confession took *cojones*. And I always wondered.

DANA

Wondered what?

LEO

Him living here all these years, never making a pass at you.

DANA

You wanted him to?!

LEO

No. *(Flustered)* It's hard to explain.

DANA

Let me guess. You wanted "the world's greatest lover" to validate your taste.

> LEO *nods sheepishly.*

You . . . would.

> *The doorbell rings.*

LEO

Who the F.? *(He opens the door, and there is MR. JACK.)* She dumped you *already?!*

MR. JACK

I can't stay there tonight. Violetta's sleeping over.

LEO

So talk about chutzpah, you come back here?

MR. JACK

Where else could I go?

LEO

They've got this new invention, it's called a hotel!

MR. JACK

It's late, I don't have much cash —

LEO

Oh, Christ, come on in.

MR. JACK

I'll be gone first thing tomorrow, I promise.

LEO

You bet your ass! And stay away from my scotch. *(Starts upstairs, pauses.)* Dah-nah?

DANA

I'll be right up.

> LEO, *not liking her answer, goes upstairs.*

DANA

Didn't think you could pull it off! A handful of spit! How can anyone be so gullible?

MR. JACK

One . . . wonders.

DANA

(After a sharp look which he pretends not to notice) I'm going to get you back.

MR. JACK

No, you won't.

DANA

Tell you why. You only want what you can't have. When you get it, you don't want it any more. Also — you know the difference between prime and McDonald's.

MR. JACK

Don't you understand? For the first time in my life, I *need* to be needed.

DANA

I need you!

> LEO *reappears, unnoticed.*

MR. JACK

No, you don't. To extend your food analogy, I was your marriage's Hamburger Helper. Leo is vital to you. He looks at you as if he won the lottery. *You* need that. Which is why every time we made love, you stared past me. Through me. And I knew what were you seeing, in your mind's eye.

DANA

Don't go there . . . please.

LEO

(Entering) Oooooh, no! You'd *better* go there!

DANA

How long have you been listening?

LEO

Long enough. So what *was* she staring at?

MR. JACK

Her guilt. Staring into the heart of it. That's why I could never come, Leo. I know too much about not being able to say I love you.

> LEO *thinks it over; then pours a*
> *scotch, which he passes to* MR.
> JACK.

MR. JACK

What's this for?

LEO

(Approaching DANA) Is he right?

> DANA *doesn't trust herself to*
> *reply. She slumps against* LEO
> *and begins to cry. Or seems to.*

Hey-y-y, it's OK . . . don't cry, baby . . . it's OK.

> *They kiss.* MR. JACK *steps*
> *forward, glass in hand, and ad-*
> *dresses the audience.*

MR. JACK

Some second-stage romantics never go on to the third stage. They
slip right back into the first. *(Staring somberly into his glass)* Wish I
could do that.

> *Still kissing* LEO, DANA *lets*
> *one hand stray to* MR. JACK*'s*
> *thigh. He tries to brush it away,*
> *but loses the battle, raises it to*
> *his lips, kisses her fingertips . . .*
> *then gives them a sharp nip. She*
> *yelps and pulls hand back.*

> MR. JACK *steps away.*

LEO *(Startled)*

What? I hurt you?

DANA

A little. (*Seductive glance at MR. JACK*) But that's not necessarily a bad thing . . .

CURTAIN

AFTERWORD

MISTER JACK'S TECHNIQUE FOR
LOOKING AT WOMEN

In the second act lecture to an audience allegedly only consisting of men, Mister Jack, when challenged to explain some of his seduction techniques, says that he sometimes employs "a stare I learned from a hypnotist," at which point he is interrupted by Leo, who says, "To learn how to stare like Mr. Jack, buy a copy of *Mr. Jack -- For Better or For Worse,* on sale in the lobby of this theatre."

The astute reader will already have discovered our protagonist's technique in a first act stage direction, but if you are like me and tend to skim swiftly through stage directions, you may have missed it, so here it is again –

In this sequence, MR. JACK reveals his skill as a seducer. He lowers his voice, takes "her" hand and talks to "DOMINIQUE" as if the audience did not exist.

He never takes his eyes off "her", and uses the hypnotist's trick of seeming to look into "her"eyes, but really staring at a point in mid-forehead and an inch within, as if he had X-ray vision.

Some hypnotists do indeed use this subtly unsettling device.

www.ingramcontent.com/pod-product-compliance
Lightning Source LLC
La Vergne TN
LVHW011202080426
835508LV00007B/556